Second Edition

FOREVER GREEN

*The History and Hope of
the American Forest*

CHUCK LEAVELL

with MARY WELCH

MERCER
Mercer University Press
Macon

FOREVER
GREEN

Published by
Evergreen Arts
665 Charlane Drive
Dry Branch, Georgia 31020

Distributed by
Mercer University Press
6316 Peake Road
Macon, Georgia 31210

Printed in the United States of America

1st printing, 2001, 2nd printing 2003
Library of Congress Catalog Number: 00-112263
ISBN: 086554-900-1

Cover and book design by Burtch Bennett Hunter
Book production by Jill Dible

To my wonderful wife Rose Lane
and our beautiful daughters Amy and Ashley.
May we always remember our ties and
responsibility to the Earth, and let us
strive to be the best stewards
of the land we can be.

ACKNOWLEDGMENTS

If someone had told me 20 years ago that I would one day be writing a book on forestry, I would have said that they were completely nuts. But fate has a way of playing funny tricks on us, and what once seemed impossible can become reality. One thing for sure is that I could never have done this alone, and I am truly grateful for all of those that have helped and encouraged me to complete this project.

In the early summer of 1998, I was about to embark on the European portion of the "Bridges To Babylon" tour as keyboardist with the Rolling Stones. In order to keep myself busy during the "down times," I thought about doing some writing. Since the only thing I know much about other than music is my passion for trees and forestry, I decided that would be the focus of my efforts. I first created an outline of my thoughts, and then began to fill in the outline as the tour progressed. At the end of the "Babylon" tour, the Stones decided to continue to work, and with a live CD out called *No Security*, we came back to America in early 1999 to play indoor arenas and then finalized the tour with a select few dates in Europe.

I continued to work on my book, and when the tour finished, I realized that I needed help to bring it all together. I needed to enlist someone who could articulate my thoughts, do some research, and help me to make sense out of the whole thing. Mary Welch had done an article on me for *South* magazine a couple of years before the "Babylon" tour, and I had been impressed with the way she put the article together. My friend and public relations coordinator, Dan Beeson, suggested that I contact her, and as soon as we met I had a good feeling that she could grasp what I was trying to do. The next step was for her to come down to our place, Charlane Plantation, to talk to us about how we got into all of this, and to gain a better understanding of our passion for trees and forests. I then gave her all that I had written, and she began to do the research, and the collaboration was born. I don't think anyone else in the whole world could have been more pleasant to work with, and no one could have done a better job than she. Thanks, Mary!

There are really not enough words in the English language to say what my wife, Rose Lane, and my daughters, Amy and Ashley, mean to me. They are my life, and my utmost passion. When I fell in love with Rosie, I had no idea that that love would lead to another . . . a love of the land. Her family, going back as many generations as we can find, has been devoted to working and preserving the land. Through farming, managing their forestland, managing wildlife species and other endeavors, they have been exemplary stewards of their land, and have helped countless others to learn the art of good stewardship. It is their heritage, and now it is my own, and our children's. We are fortunate beyond words to be able to live on and work not only the land that has been passed down to us, but additional land that we have been able to aquire on our own.

Family values run strong in the genes of the Faulks, Densons, Whites, and Leavells, and I must thank those in these families who have helped shape those values. My own mother and father, Frances H. and Billy Leavell, were my main role models, and although both are departed from this

Earth, I consider myself the luckiest guy in the world to be their son. My brother Billy and my sister Judy have both been strong and positive influences on me, and I owe them a great deal for their love and guidance of their baby brother.

My mother-in-law, Rosaline Denson White, has become my matriarchal influence since the death of my own mother, and she has helped to raise and influence our children much for the better. She has also been a source of strength to me personally, and has showed me the value of not giving up on love. Alton V. White III, my brother-in-law, took this city boy into the world of the great outdoors. He showed me how to drive a tractor and maintain it, how to hunt, and how to appreciate the woods in a way I never had before. He also must be the most fair and even-handed person I've ever known. Mary Dykes, our aunt, the sister of Rose Lane's father, has been the best source of historic information on our family and our area, as well as a loving and caring person to all who know her. Rose Lane's father, Alton V. White II, whom I knew for only a short time, as he passed away during our first year of marriage, was nonetheless a great influence on me. He accepted a rather suspect outsider – and perhaps worse, a musician – into his family, and made me feel a part of it from the beginning. To all of the above, and to all of their family members, my heartfelt and never-ending thanks for your love and inspiration.

There are many others who have contributed to this endeavor, and to my love of forestry, and there is a story behind each one . . . but that's another book! So instead of telling all the tales here, I have chosen to name them on the following pages, and it is with sincere gratitude to each and every one that I acknowledge their support, contributions, and encouragement. Thanks, guys!

Zell Miller
Former President Jimmy Carter
Blake Sullivan
Joy Hulgan
John Yow
Burtch Hunter
Robyn Richardson
Jill Dible
Al Goetzl
Flournoy Holmes
Scott Bard
Barbara Babbit Kaufman
Marc Jolley
Bob Simpson
Larry Wiseman
Sue Shaddeau
Vanessa Bullwinkle
American Forest Foundation
American Tree Farm System®
Fred Whyte
Gary Hardee
Deb Thomas
Peter Burton
Ken Waldron
Andreas Stihl
Stihl Inc.®
Arthur Temple
Brenda Elliott
Jay Brittain
Temple-Inland Company
Jonathan Gerland
Patsy Colbert
Steven Anderson
Cheryl Oakes

Forest History Society
Bob Izlar
Kris Irwin
Mike Zupko
April Lavender
Homer Rawles
Dr. Arnett Mace
Georgia Forest Association
Yale School of Forestry
Dan Beeson
Ken Willis
GCI/Atlanta
Sharon Freeman
Bob Morrison
Roger Cortoni
Bessie Williams
Jim Curry
Herman Robertson
Alphonsi Robertson
Mike Wilbanks
Jack Proctor
Marc Smith
Charles and Larry Hill
Hill Brothers Logging
Skoots Lyndon
Steve and Maritsa Bell
J. D. and Gail Bearrentine
Jason Howard
National Arbor Day Foundation
Fred Allen
Twiggs County Forestry Unit
Mike Hattaway
Marc Jolley
Mercer University Press

FROM MARY WELCH:

First, I'd like to thank Chuck and Rose Lane Leavell for taking a city girl into their home and teaching me about the magical world of trees. They have been supportive, hospitable and a joy.

I'd also like to thank my husband, Ralph McGill Jr., my best friend, soul mate and the best writer I know, as well as our son, Grady Welch McGill, who introduced me to the indescribable pleasures of being a mom. To my mother, Mary Passamano Welch, my brother Harold and his wife, Betsie, and my other brother Frank and his wife, Leah, as well as to other family members, friends and associates, thank you for letting me gush about Chuck and the book over the last several months.

And, finally to Beaver, a beloved 10-year-old golden retriever, who every night would sleep at my feet while I worked on the book. Beaver is now in the great forest in the sky where everything is Forever Green.

CONTENTS

FOREWORD

Chuck Leavell has written a heartfelt appreciation of our forest resource heritage. In it, he tells us of his beloved 2,000-acre Charlane Plantation in Twiggs County, Georgia. It is a story of our heritage, our relationship to the land, and our responsibility to be good stewards of our nation's forests.

His book gives a broad overview of world forest types, uses of forest products, regional forest history and personal examples from national award-winning Charlane Plantation.

Forest products touch our lives every day. Sure, we know about paper and lumber, but what about cancer drugs, toothpaste, football helmets, paint thinner and the literally hundreds of other common products derived from trees? In Chuck's case, it is the magnificent piano with its wooden case, striking hammers and soundboard. Our connection to and heritage from the forest are very real.

Chuck Leavell is proud of his forest heritage and what his forest means to his family.

Chuck's global music career has given him unusual wisdom and an appreciation for balance. Chuck advocates a reasoned approach to natural resource use and the sometimes contentious debate surrounding using our forest resources.

Chuck Leavell is a professional to the core. Whether he is playing beautiful music before a crowd of thousands or working his land, he gets involved. He gets dirty. He pays attention. He speaks from the heart.

His love of music and the land is genuine. He is superbly

adept at the keyboards, and he is equally proficient managing his land and being a spokesman for sound, sustainable forest resource management. Chuck Leavell is a leader in the music world and in forestry because he works hard, learns his material and practices until everything he does is natural and "forever green."

— ZELL MILLER, United States Senate

PREFACE
TO THE SECOND EDITION

$\rightharpoonup$

Chuck and Rose Lane Leavell have a wonderful vision of the future of our country. They have reverence for the God-given beauty of nature exemplified in the trees that abound on their farmland. They have described the remarkable atmospheric cleansing power of their trees. They take pride in the prospect that some of their trees will be transformed by skilled craftsmen into houses and handsome furniture. They have demonstrated that well managed forests can mean profitable family farms, even at a time when a decreasing number of farms in our country can produce only modest returns on invested capital, quite apart from supporting a middle class standard of living.

Chuck Leavell and I have enjoyed very different careers. He has established a world-famous reputation as a gifted musician, and I have had the opportunity to represent the people of Indiana in the United States Senate since 1977. But many of our best common aspirations and values have been bolstered by a common source. We are both strong family men who had the good fortune to inherit farmland and to find talented foresters and soil and water conservation leaders. We learned the excitement of timber stand improvement as we cut the vines that choked some of our most beautiful trees and liberated the crowns of these trees as they strove for the daylight. We planted thousands of seedlings and nurtured small trees with recognition that harvest of the best of these was decades away. And year after year, we pruned and shaped our young trees and tried to cut back the natural ground vegetation or unforgiving outlaw trees that might inhibit the growth and health of our favored young.

We continued to extract all the wisdom that we could glean from the forestry experts and from our own "hands-on" experiences in days of working with our trees. We grew in our understanding of the myriad ways in which nature works on a single tree. We witnessed the activities of the birds and the animals who also enjoyed the shelter and the nourishment provided by our trees. Inevitably, we wanted to tell our families and our friends — and then a much wider circle of people — about the tree farm experience and all that it might mean in the enrichment of their lives.

Chuck Leavell is one of our champions in the American Tree Farm System. It is now our good fortune that he has authored a book in which he has organized forestry history, described his own passionate advocacy of trees, and provided enjoyable and friendly advice for a growing audience who want to share the tree farming experiences that have enriched the lives of Chuck and Rose Lane Leavell.

The Lugar Farm covers 604 acres in the southwest part of Indianapolis-Marion County in central Indiana. Our 200 acres of trees combined with equal acreages of corn and soybeans are an exciting challenge for me but modest in comparison with the Leavell's Charlane Plantation in Twiggs County, Georgia. I have entertained a national convention of the Walnut Council, forestry experts from many countries, and governmental forestry leaders from our own country to provide substantial support to all who have enthusiasm for trees.

But I applaud Chuck Leavell for constructing a much better "soapbox" for advancing wisdom about trees and the ways in which our experiences with them can enrich our lives and enlarge our understanding of who we are and what we should be doing with the precious time each one of us is given. His book, "Forever Green," will inform and inspire. It will be the permanent testimony of one who was impelled to spread the good news of his trees and their transforming power in shaping his constructive life.

— U.S. SENATOR DICK LUGAR
Former Chairman of the Senate Agriculture, Nutrition and Forestry Committee

INTRODUCTION

by ROSE LANE LEAVELL

"He who plants a tree plants a hope."
~ Lucy Larcom

My family has been living on the land here in Georgia since the 1700s, when King George V made a land grant to the Faulk family. When I was a young girl growing up on my mom and dad's farm, my grandmother, Miss Julia Faulk White, lived nearby on land that my grandfather, Alton V. White Sr., bought sometime in the 1930s.

Granddaddy attended the University of Georgia, studying agriculture and forestry, and eventually went into the timber business. He passed away in 1954, and while I remember him pretty well, I spent more time with my grandmother, who lived until 1981.

Like Granddaddy, my grandmother came from a farming background; one year she even won a state competition for peanuts. Together she and Granddaddy farmed the land, and they loved it. They oversaw a diverse farming operation that included row crops, cattle, hay fields and timber.

Because my father had predeceased her, my grandmother left me the homeplace when she died. The house had been built around 1870 and began as a simple wooden "bayou style" farmhouse with "dogtrots" in the front and back. It's a wonderful home, with both the exterior and interior walls made of wood, most of it from trees that grew on our land. It goes without saying that they don't make houses like that anymore.

Of course, through the years, it has been added on to — by the Everett family, who were the original builders, by my grandmother, and by Chuck and me.

To pick up that part of the story, Chuck and I had our first date on New Year's Eve, 1972, in New Orleans. The Allman Brothers were playing a place called the Warehouse there, and the band was doing the first nationwide radio simulcast. At the time, I was one of the few employees of Capricorn Records and had worked hard on that project.

Chuck had been in the studio with the Brothers recording the legendary record *Brothers and Sisters*, which became the best-selling album of that year. Among the hits on that album was "Jessica," an instrumental piece written by Dickey Betts that showcased Chuck, only 20 years old at the time, as one of the most talented pianists in rock music.

The band wanted to take a break from the studio and play a few concerts, highlighted by the New Orleans date. Due to the broadcast, I was attending the concert, and Chuck asked me to go to dinner with him one night. We clicked immediately, and after that we only had time for each other and our mutual love of music.

After our marriage in June 1973, we traveled extensively on various tours with the Brothers, even after our first child Amy was born in 1975. We were like musical gypsies, carrying Amy around from gig to gig. Of course, as the Allman Brothers became one of the biggest bands in the world, the accommodations and touring style quickly improved. Overnight, it seems, we went from buses to private planes.

The Allman Brothers temporarily disbanded in 1976, so Chuck, Jaimoe (drummer), and Lamar Williams (bassist) from the Brothers, along with Jimmy Nalls, who had played guitar with Chuck during his earlier work with both Alex Taylor and Dr. John, formed a new band called Sea Level. The band had quite a cult following that continues to this day. While the five Sea Level albums were deemed "critical successes," and sold reasonably well, the band never exactly became a household word. Eventually Capricorn Records, which recorded most of these bands, went bankrupt. Sea Level went on to record for a short time with Arista Records before breaking up in 1980.

At this time, the Leavell family consisted of the two of us plus Amy, our seven-year-old (our second daughter Ashley was born in 1982, when Chuck was touring with the Rolling Stones). I was running a women's clothing store in Macon called Cornucopia – funded, by the way, from a timber sale on some land that my deceased father had left to my brother, Alton V. White III, and me.

Chuck was – in polite terms – in between musical gigs. Frankly, he had no job to speak of — except yard work — and there wasn't enough yard to keep him busy. So we switched roles for a while, with me working and Chuck staying at home looking after Amy and the house, and even doing some of the cooking.

One day I came home and saw that the latest edition of *Southern Living* had come in the mail. On the cover was a beautiful strawberry shortcake. And on my kitchen table was — surprise! — a beautiful strawberry shortcake. Chuck had spent the entire afternoon making a strawberry shortcake from the *Southern Living* recipe.

I looked at him and the shortcake and said firmly, "We've got to get you something else to do."

As fate would have it, my grandmother, Miss Julia, passed way in 1981 and we moved to her house in the country. Little did we know how our lives would change . . . and little did we know that trees and forestry would become the main component of that change. Suddenly we were Tree Farmers, and I guess that all things come to pass for a reason. Chuck took to it with all his heart! He never does anything without tremendous conviction and passion.

Not that it was easy. The move from the comforts of a modern home to an old house in the country, the beginning of an entirely new kind of work, the uncertainty of Chuck's musical career – all made for somewhat tough times. But they were also very wonderful times, and we became a stronger family for all that we went through. Thank God Chuck didn't sell his piano, because Mick Jagger called pretty soon after that.

In fact, Chuck's work with the Rolling Stones has been good for him, for me, and for the house. After each of his tours, Chuck would promise me a new bathroom with a large tub so I could take long luxurious bubble baths. Finally, after all these years and many tours, I'm proud to say that the house now has a master bath. I'm especially proud that we sawed most of the lumber used in this and many other building projects here on the plantation. Chuck salvaged timber that had been stuck by lightning or infested with beetles and brought it up here to the house, where my brother, A. V. III, used his Woodmiser sawmill and sawed the lumber according to our needs. Once again, we were preserving our heritage, using what had been left to us by my grandparents, our land and timber, and making our home a better place for us and our children.

During the 20 years that we have resided here at Charlane Plantation (named by taking the first part of Chuck's proper name, Charles, and the second part of my name, Rose Lane), we have made our own mark on the land, the house, and the community. I believe that it has all been very positive. Along the way, we have worked hard to be good stewards of the land, something that my forefathers already knew. We have learned how and when to plant, how much of this and that makes a good crop, when to weed the garden. All the while, Chuck, in particular, has become a widely respected and award-winning forester. Who would have imagined?

. . . I will say, though, that it was a very good strawberry shortcake!

FOREVER
GREEN

CHAPTER ONE

TREES AND KEYS

"She is a tree of life to them that lay hold upon her:
and happy is everyone that retaineth her."
~ Proverbs 3:18

I am a musician by trade. My friends say I am a tree farmer in my heart and a musician in my soul. The piano was my first instrument. My mother played the piano, and as a young boy growing up in Tuscaloosa, Alabama, I learned to play by imitating her, starting when I was about six years old. I believe that is the way most of us really learn – first by imitating and then experimenting on our own.

I was lucky. My mom taught me early on that more important than the notes played on an instrument are the emotions and feelings being expressed. "Chuck," she would ask, "what would it sound like if there was a storm brewing?" And I would rumble something low on the keyboard. Or she might ask how would it sound if I just felt fantastic and it was a beautiful day, and I would try to play out that feeling. It was a very valuable lesson, one that I still try to remember when I play. When I was about 10, I took up the guitar and went through the whole folk craze of the early 1960s: Chad and Jeremy, The

Kingston Trio, The New Christy Minstrels, Bob Dylan. When folk faded and rock 'n' roll came into our world – Chuck Berry, Elvis, The Beatles, The Rolling Stones – I took a turn at the drums and other instruments. I even played the tuba in my junior high school band for two years.

But my first and true love is for that marvelous acoustic wonder, the grand piano. For me there is nothing that is quite so wonderful, so amazing, so musically capable of such expression and emotion. A piano can be playful, majestic, whimsical, serious, funny, serene, restless. A song played on the piano can be loud and brash, soft and comforting, silky smooth and sexy or hard and independent. Really, any state of mind you can think of can be expressed by playing this incredible instrument.

It is also pleasing to the eye. To me, there is nothing quite so beautiful as the shape of a grand piano. Its stateliness, its curve, the way the lid opens up to reveal the strings and pins of the harp that shine and sparkle in the light . . . the contrast of the black and white keys that beg to be touched, caressed and explored. I know this may sound like words from a romance novel, but I believe every one of them.

And I'm not alone.

Joni Mitchell, the great Canadian singer-songwriter, wrote about expressing one's feelings on the piano in her song, "Ludwig's Tune":

> *. . . condemned to wires and hammers*
> *strike every chord that you feel*
> *that broken trees and elephant ivories conceal.*

Such beautiful words, and for me, that just about says it all. Broken trees, yes, but so carefully and artfully broken, then crafted into an exquisite marvel.

Growing up in Alabama the son of an insurance salesman, I never dreamed I'd be talking about touching and caressing a piano. But the piano is a wondrous instrument that has given me my livelihood, provided for my family, given me so much joy and allowed me to express my own feelings.

And growing up in Alabama, I never thought much about trees and their place in the world. Back in junior high school huffing into that tuba, I couldn't have said which would be the more unreal dream – becoming a musician and playing with some of the best bands in the world or being a tree farmer. Both have come true, and both have taken me on long, winding, and wonderful paths.

Truth be told, in my early years I didn't really understand and fully appreciate the music I was playing. Only years later did I come to realize where my music was coming from: those blues musicians who played on street corners and in dives across the South; the gospel music, both black and white, that I heard on the radio on Sunday mornings; the piano styles of Jerry Lee Lewis and Little Richard. It came from Mississippi Fredd McDowell, Muddy Waters, Howlin' Wolf, Robert Johnson, Otis Span, Memphis Slim, Little Walter, and especially Ray Charles. Later on, inspiration came from artists like Nicky Hopkins, Leon Russell, Elton John, Keith Jarrett, Chick Corea, Joe Zawinul and so many others. All these great musicians — and all the ones whose names won't ever be known — melded mysteriously and gave me my sound.

Years ago Keith Richards wanted to do a tribute to one of his idols, Chuck Berry. Keith put together a band – and I was honored to be among the members – that worked with Chuck and Keith on a movie, *Hail, Hail Rock and Roll.* It was Keith's way to paying a debt to the musicians who had come before and had such great influence.

It took years before I realized and recognized the value of

the legacy of those musicians, so I knew exactly where Keith was coming from. And only by understanding where the music came from can we learn to bend it, massage it, alter it and move it forward. And to think I was just trying to sound like the "British Invasion" bands!

It's the same with trees. When Rose Lane and I married, I learned to know and love trees when we would take walks through her family's land. Her brother took me fishing and hunting, and I was hooked on the rural outdoor life. There was no way we were going to move to Nashville, New York, Miami, Los Angeles, or any big city to further my musical career. We were staying on the farm.

But music was my life, and it never occurred to either of us that trees would become not only our passion but our livelihood — just as music was.

In 1981, Rose Lane inherited 1200 acres of land and a house from her grandmother. The property was originally purchased by her grandfather, Alton V. White Sr., a half-century earlier. Mr. White had studied at the University of Georgia, in part concentrating on forestry, and eventually went into business buying and selling tracts of land and timber. This particular tract caught Mr. White's eye, as it was only a few miles from where he lived in middle Georgia, and he purchased it for just a few dollars per acre, maybe $5 or less. But remember that this was a long time ago, so it probably amounted to a tidy sum.

His wife, Miss Julia, came from a farming and cattle background, and was engaged in running that aspect of their land. Now as they already had a home not too far away from this new acquisition, they didn't move there to begin with. At this time they had their two children, a son, Alton Jr. (Rose Lane's father, now deceased), and a daughter Mary, who still lives in the area. One great story from Aunt Mary is that when they first bought this place, Miss Julia would get up early in the morning, leaving Mary in the care of a maid, and take a horse and buggy with little Al in it to the new farm. She would either put little Al in the care of one of the hands to look after him, or sometimes take him with her on the rounds, and she would direct the farming activities for the course of the day, returning home sometimes after dark in that horse and buggy rig.

It wasn't until some time in the '30s that they decided to make the move to this new property. The place had an old house on it, and they had to do some work to fix it up. Money was tight – this was the Depression, after all – but they managed to make some improvements, moved the family there and dubbed it Whiteway Farms. They had to work very hard for what they had, but they were making it. This was the rural South – dirt roads, the only telephone at the community store – but they made a good life. They worked the land, raised their children, and became pillars of the community. They were active in their church, Richland Baptist. They were well respected, and had many friends and relatives in the area.

Horseback riding – both for transportation and for sport – was an essential aspect of life during these times, and Miss Julia and Mr. Al enjoyed their horses just as Rose Lane and I do today. One of the main social events of the times was fox hunting, and Mr. White at one time had more than 100 fox hounds – some of them world class – out in a big pen in the backyard. Other men sought him out to breed their dogs to his. I can just imagine the scene when they would turn those dogs loose for the hunt. Miss Julia and Mr. Al – or "Chief," as many called him – galloping through the woods with all of their friends on a beautiful misty country morning, dew still on the ground, the sun filtering through the trees, the horses dancing over the ravines and ditches, the dogs racing through the trees in pursuit of the fox, howling and baying . . . an occasional deer or two jumping up from their bedding place, disturbed with all the excitement . . . perhaps a covey of quail flushing unexpectedly and surprising the riders and horses. What a scene it must have been!

This is a time long gone now, and nowadays hunting is for game for the table. But of course some of the flavor of that life still exists today. Rose Lane and I still enjoy our land for recreational use like her grandmother and grandfather did, and I am convinced that they are smiling down on us as we do.

We knew that Rose Lane would eventually inherit the land, but we didn't give it much thought. We were living comfortably in our second home in Macon, Georgia, and my career was going fine. When Miss Julia passed away, it was a shock and a wake-up call all at once. First, we had lost a loved one, and it was difficult to think of anything else. Then came some surprises. The first surprise was from the Internal Revenue Service. This was back in the early '80s, when interest rates were around 18-20 percent, and estate taxes were much worse than they are now. The exemption was relatively small compared to what it is today. We even had to sell some of Rose Lane's land in order to make the first payment to the IRS. It took us 15 years to pay off the entire tax bill, but we did it . . . we had to.

There were other problems. Miss Julia had been ill the last several years of her life, and had not been able to run the place like I know she would have liked. The house was in dire need of repairs. We had to re-wire, re-plumb, refurbish and just about rebuild the whole place. The barns and other outbuildings were run down, too. And as Miss Julia had to have money to live on, from time to time she would sell some timber for income. Unfortunately, some of the timber was "high-graded," meaning that the best and most valuable timber was cut, and

Rose Lane's grandparents, Miss Julia and Mr. Al.

the crooked and diseased trees, which had much lower value, were for the most part the ones that were left.

Once we had dealt with some of these painful realities, we had to decide what to do with the land. I had started touring with several bands again, and my musical career prevented me from farming annual crops that had a definite planting and harvesting season. Cattle farming would have required too much day-to-day attention, and I had no real knowledge of farming or raising cattle. I considered other options, like pecan groves, peach trees, nursery stock and such, but somehow they didn't really seem right. Then one day while sitting at the kitchen table discussing the problem, Rose Lane's brother, Alton White III, suggested we revive her grandfather's love of forestry and grow trees for production of pulp and saw timber.

It was the perfect solution. We could grow, manage and harvest trees, but I could still record or be on the road for months at a time playing music with artists like the Rolling

Stones, Eric Clapton, George Harrison, The Indigo Girls and some of the others I've had the privilege to work with.

But I had a lot to learn. When we created Charlane Plantation as a tree farm back in 1981, I hadn't really given much thought to trees and their role in our lives. They were, well, just trees! So I began to research the subject of trees and forests and forest management. I went to the library and checked out books. I attended seminars on managing timber and wildlife. I sought out others that I knew I could learn from. I went to the Forest Commission office in my area and got pamphlets and other literature. I went to other government agricultural agencies, like the ASCS office, the Soil and Water Conservation office to investigate programs and to get advice. Eventually I enrolled in a correspondence course that was offered by the Forest Landowners Association and the Georgia Extension Service. It was a well-written and well-organized course, and I learned a great deal from it. At the time I was on tour with the Fabulous Thunderbirds, a blues band from Texas, and I managed to do my homework on our tour bus, or in my hotel room, or backstage on breaks. To finish the course, I was required to write a management plan for our property. I did this with some help from a consulting forester, and then began to implement the plan around 1985.

All of this set me on a journey – a wonderful journey that I had no idea I was to take, but one that I am so grateful to have traveled. And the journey continues. I have learned a great deal – about biodiversity, about our ecosystem, about wildlife management and habitat. I've seen the effects of good, sound stewardship and good management practices. I've learned how to work with nature, to be patient and not get in too much of a hurry in these things. I've learned that the more you learn, the more there is to learn. And I've learned a lot about myself, by taking long walks in the woods, and having time to spend in nature with my own thoughts and psyche.

I think the most important thing I have learned is that there is a delicate balance in our world, and it's up to us to understand that balance and work to keep it in place. And it is my mission to maintain and even improve that balance on Charlane Plantation, and to try to help others understand how we can maintain that balance in our country, in our world, and still make good use of our most precious natural resource. I have grown to have a great admiration and wonder of forests and their spirit — and for tree farmers!

Without knowing and appreciating where our music comes from, we can't create new sounds. Similarly, if we don't understand the value of trees and what they mean to our lifestyle, our past and our future, we then won't be able to fully use their potential or prepare our forests for future generations. And that would threaten our very existence. Forest management can be a controversial subject. Good forest and land stewardship can take different forms for different parts of the world, but without a doubt it is the key to keeping our forests and agricultural lands healthy. In this book I want to explore this idea, and to show that we can indeed have healthy forests and still continue to have the wonderful gifts that trees give us. We will look at where we've been in America with our forests . . . and at the changes, both good and bad, that have occurred with them throughout our history. And we'll take a realistic look at where we are and where we are going. I think it is a wonderful and interesting story, and as the title of this book suggests, a story of hope.

CHAPTER TWO

⌒

THE GIFTS OF THE FOREST

*"The cultivation of trees is the cultivation of the good,
the beautiful and the ennobling in man."*
~ J. Sterling Morton

The late, great children's author Shel Silverstein wrote a book, *The Giving Tree*, that tells the story of a boy who befriends a tree and eventually uses up all of it for the many things in his life. He uses it to play under, to build a tree house, and when older, to carve his and his girlfriend's initials in. Still later, he cuts the tree down to build a house. When the boy grows into an old man and is tired, feeble and looking for a place to rest, he finally winds up sitting on its stump with the tree's permission. It's a wonderful book, and I hope that if you haven't already read it to your kids, you will take the time to find it and do so.

Our forests have always given us so much and continue giving. If you look at what a tree is made of, you'll find that every part plays a role in our everyday lives.

A tree is made up of at least half water. Once a tree is cut down, it becomes dry. Dry wood consists of five other components: cellulose, hemicellulose, lignin, tall oil, and turpentine. Each of these is used either in the paper-making process or in making chemicals, or else sold for other purposes.

Cellulose is needed to make paper. It also is used for diapers, plastics, overhead transparencies and even in screwdriver handles. Cellulose derivatives are also used in some food products, like salad dressings and Parmesan cheese.

Hemicellulose are the sugars in the wood. We all know that the maple syrup we put on our pancakes comes from trees. But sap from other trees is used to make paint thinners, turpentine, perfume and xylitol, an artificial sweetener found in some chewing gums. It can also be burned for fuel and fermented into ethanol.

Lignin, the "glue" that holds the cellulose fibers in the tree together, is used in polychemicals.

Tall oil is in the tree's sap and an essential ingredient for oleochemicals, which are used in oil-based paints and in some new products designed to lower cholesterol. It's also used in soaps and detergents, tires, and corrosion inhibitors for coating pipes.

Turpentine provides flavors in foods and fragrances, such as in citronella candles. Wood fiber is used to make products like plastic filler, chemicals, shoe polish, toothpaste, varnish, foam rubber and much more. Other wood-fiber byproducts of the milling process are used to fuel electrical generators to run factories. Tree bark is used in landscape mulch, soil conditioners, medicines and cosmetics.

Even a tree's sawdust is useful. Sawdust is the starting point for making activated carbon, which can absorb gases. Sawdust can be used for purification purposes, such as water filters and gas masks. If your car has an emissions-control canister that collects evaporated gas, then your car has sawdust in it.

Just look around. Trees are everywhere. Most of the acoustic instruments that we so deeply and dearly love to hear and play couldn't exist without wood. My beloved piano is made in large part from wood. Maple and spruce are two of the species often used in grand pianos – maple for the case and spruce for the soundboard. The guitar, mandolin, violin, viola, cello, contra-basses, drums, and clarinet are among the other instruments made from various wood species – maple, mahogany, rosewood, sycamore, spruce, and ebony, along with other more exotic woods. While other components like strings, metal parts, skins or plastic help make each instrument's characteristic sounds, wood still is the basic material in all these instruments.

Throughout the world and time, civilizations have made musical instruments from wood. The Aborigines of northern Australia play the didgeridoo, a natural trumpet made from termite-hollowed eucalyptus branches. Those who remember songs from the 1960s will remember the folk song, "Tie Me Kangaroo Down, Sport" and its chorus, "Play your didgeridoo, blue." Russians play the lojki or wooden spoons to keep a beat. In Venezuela, they play the quitaiplas, which are made from bamboo and when hit against the floor produce a unique "qui-tai-pla" sound. The Japanese play a shakuhachi, a bamboo flute (technically bamboo is a grass, but still worth noting, and many other Japanese instruments are made from wood), while in Tahiti, a to'ere is played, which is a split log drum.

I can't even imagine what type of mind it took to come up with some of the wonderful uses for trees. Take paper, for instance. The early Egyptians used papyrus, a grass-like plant, to make paper. But paper as we know it today originated in China around 105 AD. What made someone look at a tree and invent the whole concept of paper and writing on it? Some of the great political and religious revolutions took hold because paper and the printing press were available so that masses of people could read the ideas and take action.

But even if civilizations didn't have paper, they used trees to tell their stories. Tribes such as the Haida Indians in Alaska used totem poles—great carved trunks of wood—to tell the story of a family, a god or an individual. In some cultures, when a family's chief died, his heirs were responsible for erecting a memorial pole that displayed the crests and important events in the deceased's family. Tribes in Alaska and the Pacific Northwest were not the only people to use wood to communicate. Tribes in Africa, Australia, South America and Polynesia all carved images in masks and poles. When the word had to spread quickly and far, tree trunks were used as drums to get the message out.

Think of where sports would be without wood. There would be no baseball or cricket bats, no original golf clubs, and no polo and croquet mallets. While much of modern day sports equipment is made of composites and other high-tech material, the originals were all made of wood, and in many cases still are. Even football helmets and other protective headgear in sports contain cellulose derivatives. What about our childhood toys? Today children play with Thomas the Tank Engine and Brio train sets, all made from wood. Their first exposure to the mystical principle of flying is first learned through a paper airplane made by Dad or a 59-cent balsam airplane bought at the drug store. Tree houses and doll houses helped spur our imagination and fantasy.

Trees have traditionally played a major role in folk medicine, but now pharmaceutical companies are learning the secrets of the trees, roots, leaves and berries that Native American medicine men, folk doctors and midwives all took for granted. Right now, from 25 to 50 percent of all drugs (and their synthetic derivatives) come from the rain forests, and some estimate that number may go as high as 75 percent.

Taxol is the world's largest anti-cancer drug, used by millions to battle a variety of cancers, including breast, lung, ovarian and AIDS-related cancers. It was discovered when the U.S. National Cancer Institute started a program in 1958 to screen 35,000 plant and tree species for anti-cancer activity. Luckily for millions of cancer victims, the Pacific yew tree bark was found to have an ingredient, paclitaxel, that stopped cancerous cells from dividing.

The Chinese Rubitecan acuminata tree is being studied as a treatment for pancreatic cancer. In the 1500s, Jesuit explorers discovered a South American tree that secreted quinine from its bark. Not only does quinine help prevent malaria; it also gave us tonic, which goes so perfectly with gin and vodka!

Go into any natural food store and the shelves are lined with vitamins and herbs, many derived from trees. One of the more popular ones comes from the Ginkgo Biloba tree, which is also known as the maidenhair tree. Natural food enthusiasts use Ginkoba to boost alertness and help other mental functions. In Asian cultures, it has been used to treat coughs, allergic inflammations and circulatory disorders. Recent studies suggest it may help delay the onset of Alzheimer's disease.

We all know the benefits of vitamin C, found in oranges, lemons, grapefruits and limes. And recent scientific studies also show that drinking red cherry juice helps overcome the crippling effects of arthritis. The cryptoxanthin in mangoes, oranges and papayas seems to decrease the risk of cervical cancer.

The saw palmetto tree, which is found in the Southeastern U.S., was used by the Native Americans to treat a variety of urinary problems. A cousin of the saw palmetto, the cabbage palmetto, isn't used for medicinal purposes, but it did save Sullivan's Island, outside of Charleston, from an assault by the British during the Revolutionary War. Forewarned that the British were going to attack the island, the colonists built a fort of palmetto logs. The Redcoat warships came and fired

round after round of cannonballs but to no avail—the palmetto logs were so soft the cannonballs just sank into the
wood, doing little if any damage.

Trees certainly aren't here just for us human beings to use.
Other species need them as well. Birds, squirrels, snakes—all
sorts of animals and insects—call trees home. Beavers build
dams, and other animals use our trees for food and for protection from the elements and predators. A single fallen tree in
an ancient forest, for example, may shelter as many as 1,500
invertebrates—that's quite an apartment complex!

We all know trees play a large role in helping our environment. Shade from trees helps lower temperatures, which pre-
serves energy. Three well-placed mature trees around a house
can cut air conditioning costs by 10 to 15 percent. Trees help
clean the air we breathe by absorbing harmful carbons from
the air. One adult tree absorbs about 13 pounds of harmful
carbons a year—enough to meet the breathing needs of a family of four. When we breathe, our lungs take in oxygen and
release carbon dioxide. Trees and plants do the exact opposite.
They take in carbon and release oxygen—a process called photosynthesis. For every ton of wood a forest grows, it removes
1.47 tons of carbon dioxide and replaces it with 1.07 tons of
oxygen. The average forest absorbs and ties up 26 tons of carbon dioxide per acre per year—the same amount emitted by a
car traveling 11,300 miles. Carbon dioxide contributes heavily to global warming. Just imagine how hot and smoggy it
would be without trees taking out that carbon dioxide!

Trees also trap dust and filter pollutants. Forests collect and
filter rainwater and from it generate and store ground water.
The porous soil created by decomposing leaves, bark and tree
trunks acts as a huge sponge, absorbing water and purifying it
as it seeps into the ground, surfacing later in springs and
drilled wells. The natural aquifer of pure ground water created

by the New Jersey Pine Barrens contain 30 times more water than all the reservoirs serving New York City—and think of the cost savings! It boggles my mind to think that there is more water under the forests of this planet than in all of the earth's lakes. But it's true.

Trees also serve as a natural pesticide. For instance, the extracts from the neem tree control over 250 pests and can protect several ornamental and food crops against fungus diseases such as rusts and powdery mildew that attack leaves.

When I was touring with the Rolling Stones on the "Voodoo Lounge" tour back in 1995, I met an interesting English gentleman named Daniel Morrell at a party after one of our London Wembley Stadium shows. He had started an organization called "Future Forests" that now exists throughout Europe. Dan had a rather simple yet ingenious concept: If trees indeed perform the service of converting harmful carbons to useful oxygen, then why not approach entities that create pollution and help them offset that pollution by planting trees?

Dan partnered with the University of Edinburgh Centre for Carbon Management in Scotland, which conducts "carbon audits" by calculating the pollution particular companies and entities are causing, and then figures out how many trees would offset that pollution. He successfully convinced several corporations like Mazda and Avis to become "carbon neutral" in Europe and to help fund his organization. He also convinced several touring bands to join in and calculate the carbons emitted by their planes, buses and trucks—even the emissions caused by fans who attended the concerts. At present, Pink Floyd, the Foo Fighters, Joe Strummer, and Julian Lennon are among the many musicians that have committed their tours or albums to be carbon neutral. These artists are supporting tree planting projects to offset the CO_2 created by their tour productions or manufacture and distribution of their albums. Any company can join in, and many have. Add Fiat, Unison, and Audi Belgium to the current list of supporters.

Future Forests has been a great success in Europe. Its programs have offset 250,000 Mt of CO_2 and helped plant one million saplings. Dan and I have discussed how we might bring this concept to America. While we haven't quite fulfilled that goal yet, it is something we still desire to do, and I am confident that in time we will. If you wish to find out more about this organization, here is their contact information:

Future Forests Ltd.
4 Great James Street
London WC1N 3DB
United Kingdom

They also have an excellent website: www.futureforests.com.

So far, we've concentrated on the practical uses of trees. But there is so much more. Trees play a part in our memories and offer a definition of beauty that is hard to beat.

Try picturing a tropical vacation without palm trees. Can't do it. How about camping? Those towering pine trees and hardwoods play a vital role in the whole experience. I can't imagine my beloved South without the heady smell of the magnolia tree or the dramatic canopy of the Live Oak. And every fall, no matter where you live, you dream about the maples turning brilliant shades of red, orange and yellow. In fact, nothing defines fall as much as the colors of the trees.

Like every Southern boy, I can still conjure up the taste of my mother's peach and apple cobblers and pecan pies eaten on wooden picnic tables at the church socials. And what about the peace and serenity trees offer when we're taking a walk in a park or garden?

Many of our holidays revolve around trees. For many, the

Christmas tree is an integral part of the family celebration—in fact, Christmas trees are a part of our culture, our psyche.

Rose Lane and I actually grew and sold Christmas trees at Charlane for about 12 years. Although we don't do it any more, it really was a great experience. It's another way that trees give us so much joy. You put a tiny seedling in the ground—in our case it was Virginia pines—and you take care of it. You have to shape it, and spray it to keep it disease and insect free. Virginia pines really require a lot of work, but they make for a beautiful Christmas tree. Other species, like spruce and fir, don't need quite so much care, but most of them won't make it in the hot southern climate where I live.

At any rate, after four to six years—or six to eight or even more to have a larger tree—you have families come to pick out their Christmas tree. They bring the kids, who are all excited, and you help them select a tree, harvest and wrap it up and put it in the car or truck. It makes all the work so worthwhile. It's such a joy, and it could be a profitable business under the right circumstances. Ultimately, it wasn't the right business for us for a number of reasons, but we certainly enjoyed the experience.

The bottom line is that not a day, or indeed hardly an hour, goes by that we don't enjoy the benefit of something that comes from a tree in one form or another. Trees are a fact of life, literally and figuratively. They are so integral to and ubiquitous in our human landscape that it's, pardon the expression, hard to see the forest for the trees. But the fact is, the more we learn about these solid citizens of the earth, the more we discover how they have always been our good friends and benefactors, something our primate ancestors knew as they were swingin' around the Pleistocene, millions of years ago.

So, if our forests give us all these wonderful things, then shouldn't we give back? Not only should we, but my friends, we must! So how do we give back? What can each one of us do to make a difference in conserving our forestlands?

There are many answers to these questions, but I believe it all begins with basic understanding. What is a tree? How does it grow? What's in it? What must it have to survive and thrive? What is a forest? How did we discover all the things that come from a forest? What is the history of our forests, and how did we get to where we are today? Are our precious forests in good shape, and what might the future hold for them?

This book is designed to give you some answers and help understand the importance of these issues. While it is not a textbook, I do believe it's essential to explore some of the workings of trees and forests in order to best understand what our trees and forests are. I don't intend to be too technical, but rather to give a general understanding of trees and forests, an overall view of the history of our forests and the importance of the resource of wood. It is an attempt to present the Big Picture.

It is my sincere hope that this book will provide a better comprehension of the value of trees as well as a better appreciation of them. It is also my hope to help people understand how we can continue to use the things that trees give us without putting our forests in jeopardy.

Personally, I advocate a common sense approach to the management of our country's and the world's forests. There are places that should be preserved for aesthetics, beauty, public use, and recreation; and there are forests that should be managed for production. Some can even do all of that. Let's face it, we need wood to build our homes, produce our books, make our furniture, our musical instruments, to sit under, to help our environment, and for all the numerous uses we already have mentioned, and there is no doubt that we *can* manage our forests for all of these purposes.

Trees are like music. It's fun and soothes the soul to play an instrument alone and express oneself. Many an hour, I've poured out my emotions on the piano instead of on a psychi-atrist's couch. But it's also a lot of fun to share the tune, to take the sounds from others—to be surprised by the richness of each other's sound—musical heritages blending together, if you will. Each instrument so different, but all so important to the song.

And if one instrument is off, the entire tune is adversely affected.

And so it is with trees. Maintaining our forests requires a delicate balance, where all the players have to be playing the same tune. A few people alone can't save, conserve, and pro-tect our forests. It takes arborists, loggers, foresters, mill oper-ators, environmentalists, private landowners, wildlife enthusi-asts, teachers, craftsmen, everyday concerned citizens, compa-nies involved in forest products and forest management, and all of us to make it work out right. We can't play solo on this one, for the forests are too fragile and the stakes too high. We must all take it upon ourselves to learn about our forests and support those programs that allow us to responsibly use our trees. Only then can we be sure that we will have wonderful forests for the next generation and those to come. Each tree—each forest—has its own song and we must listen.

And while we are listening and unraveling the mysteries and gifts of the trees, we should always take a moment to sit under a tree, look up and be thankful.

CHAPTER THREE

THE NAKED TRUTH ABOUT TREES

*"The Earth brought forth vegetation, plants yielding
seed according to their own kinds, and trees bearing
fruit in which is their seed. Each according to its
kind. And God saw that it was good."*
~ Genesis 1:12

TREES: THEY'RE NOT BUSH LEAGUE.

So what exactly is a tree, anyway? While schoolchildren might
easily offer a definition, it's important to start with a common
basis for discussion.

A tree is a perennial (a plant that survives from year to year)
with woody stems that can be single-trunked, like a yellow
poplar tree, or multistemmed, like an elm. They must grow to
a minimum of 15 feet tall. The diminutive Joshua "tree" in the
California desert is, in reality, a bush. More specifically it's a
large yucca plant and a member of the lily family. (Of course
U2 fans would insist that *Joshua Tree* is also a darn good rock-
and-roll album!)

The first or oldest recorded tree fossil was discovered in
Australia. Called (by those who can actually pronounce it)
Baragwanathia longifolia, it had a single stem about one inch
in diameter covered with pointy leaves. These trees, which

appeared early in the Devonian period, more than 400 million years ago, were surrounded by other primitive flora, including liverworts, mosses and horesetails. Fish were the most highly developed animals at this time.

Conifers (trees that produce cones) began to appear about 225 million years ago and quickly grew over most of the land. While some scientists still argue the point, most agree that the earliest fossil pollen was a water lily, dating back about 140 million years, and it just might have given a Jurassic dinosaur a serious case of the sniffles.

Broadleaf trees first came onto the scene in the Cretaceous period, about 136 million years ago. Among the first were magnolia, eucalyptus, willow and larch. Soon to follow were the palms, fig, birch, oak and chestnut. Just about every tree that grows today was also alive by the Paleocene period—about 65 million years ago.

Trees are fanatical survivalists—they even wear camouflage! They can sprout up almost everywhere—including cracked urban sidewalks. Once they start growing they fight for sunlight and, not surprisingly, the healthiest and fastest-growing ones win. In some areas, one parent tree can populate an entire acre of woods. But with some species, seeds cannot germinate immediately beneath the parent tree. So the seeds must put down roots elsewhere. This helps explain why sometimes pines rise beneath oaks and why oaks grow among pines. Generations of species succeed one another in leisurely, cyclical waves.

TREES 101

Science was never my strongest subject, but I think it's important to understand what makes a tree do its thing.

Starting with bark, we all know that this is basically the tree's skin. It is made up chiefly of dead cork cells, and it helps

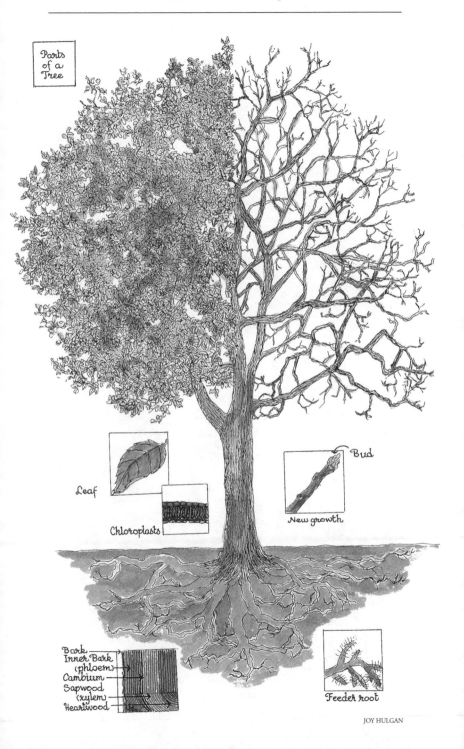

Parts of a Tree

Leaf

Chloroplasts

Bud

New growth

Bark
Inner Bark (phloem)
Cambium
Sapwood (xylem)
Heartwood

Feeder root

JOY HULGAN

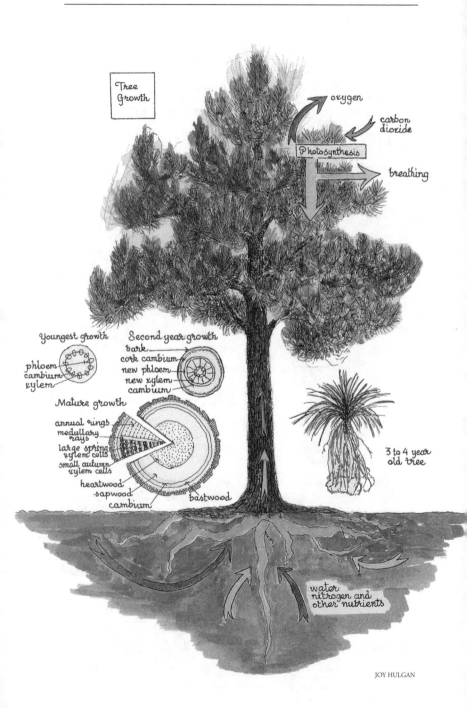

JOY HULGAN

protect the tree from disease, insects, fire and other invaders and adapts to whatever needs the tree has. For instance, the thick bark of the cork oak fights heat and dryness, while the Hawaiian Ohia Lehua's tough bark can resist the red-hot cinders from volcanic ash and fire.

If bark is the tree's frame, then the cambium is its growing tissue. It is the cambium that adds new wood cells to the circumference of the tree, layer after layer. Each year it makes new cells toward the inside and the outside. Trees are round because the cambium cells in the trunk divide at about the same time and grow at about the same rate. A tree doesn't grow more on one side than another, unless something has influenced it like wind, gravity or the sun shining more on one side than another.

The phloem cells are a layer of cells on the outside of the cambium that conduct the food-containing sap up and down the tree. They also carry sugar from the leaves and branches to supply every part of the tree with the energy it needs to live and grow.

On the inner side of the cambium is the sapwood, which is mostly made up of cells called xylem cells. The sapwood is full of tubelike structures that conduct water up from the roots to the leaves like straws. I'm sure we've all counted the lines of a tree stump, or a tree "cookie," to determine how old it was. These lines are made each year by the sapwood cells. Sapwood cells produced in the spring usually have thinner, lighter walls than those produced during the summer and fall. Thicker walls are important to help support the leaves, flowers and seeds. Together, the lighter spring cells and the darker summer-fall cells form a ring that represents a year in the life of a particular tree. At the core of the trunk is a layer called heartwood, which helps make the trunk more rigid and contains deposits of tree gums and resins.

Holding the tree in place are the roots, which vary from tree to tree. Some, like oaks, have a few strong, deep tap roots that keep the tree upright and in place. In fact, the root system in trees like the oak can spread out underground as big as the tree is above the ground. Other trees, like the poplars, have many tough, shallow roots. All trees, however, have a network of thin feeder roots that fan out just below the surface to capture water and nutrients.

AS IT LIVES AND BREATHES—A TREE'S LEAVES.

Like a tree, the leaves are a complicated factory of cells. There are two basic kinds of leaves—broadleaf and needles—or deciduous and coniferous, for the scientific-minded. Epidermal

Live Oak
Quercus virginiana

JOY HULGAN

cells, and wet-coated cells, form on the outside layer or skin of the leaf. In the broadleaf trees, the palisade layers are next. The palisade cells are the main light-capturing cells. They are full of chloroblasts, which are like little sacks containing chlorophyll. Farther into the leaf are cells that make up the veins that give the leaf its strength. Alongside the vein are spongy cells where air spaces exist. The veins supply every part of the leaf with water and chemicals.

At the bottom of the leaf is the lower skin, or epidermal cells, which are usually filled with little holes. Each hole is called a stomata, or mouth. Surrounding the stomata are guard cells. To keep all the leaf cells supplied with water, the stomata opens and closes, allowing air to come in and water vapor to go out.

Every wonder how the leaves stick to the trees? They do so with a flexible region of cells called the pulvinus. Pulvinus are fat little cells full of water than can cause the whole leaf to move slowly in a variety of directions and angles in order to better catch the sunlight.

The needles of coniferous trees are similar to the broadleaf but arranged differently. The stomata form rows running down the whole length of the needle. In the middle of the needle is a rod or two of pipeline tissues where water and food move in and out. The conifer needle has a tough layer of waxy, thick-walled cells that help make it strong enough to withstand tough winters.

Leaves have a vital function in our lives—literally for the air we breathe. Although scientists have not figured out exactly how a tree makes food, we know the recipe involves a green coloring matter called chlorophyll. Water, carbon-dioxide gas and sunlight are also added. Chlorophyll absorbs the sun's light energy and makes a special form of chemical energy that the tree can use.

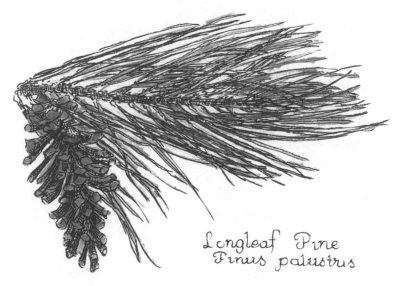

Longleaf Pine
Pinus palustris

JOY HULGAN

Chlorophyll captures as much as 2 percent of the light energy that reaches the earth. In photosynthesis, the chlorophyll puts water, carbon dioxide and light energy together to make glucose—sugar. The trees use the sugar for a variety of purposes, but mostly for food. But what is left over after photosynthesis takes place is oxygen. That's reason enough to love and protect our trees.

BENEATH THE FIG LEAF: HOW TREES DO IT.

Just like the birds and the bees and people, trees reproduce when male genetic material fertilizes a female egg. In brief, pollen grains from the male flowers drift through the air to the female flowers and unite with an egg. Some flowers are so small they're hard to see; others, like the magnolia, are quite large and beautiful. Pollen can also be brought to the female flowers by insects such as bees, by birds such as hummingbirds and by animals such as bats. Many tree species have male and female flowers on the same tree. Others have male and female trees.

The top of the female part of the flower is sticky. When the pollen grain adheres to this part, it is transported down a tube to an egg cell. The fertilized egg, called an embryo, plus a supply of stored food and a protective coat, becomes a seed. Within the seed, the embryo forms into a complete plant. Meanwhile, the seed is waiting for the right time to settle into the ground and grow into a tree. When the seed sprouts, the tiny plant emerges complete with roots and a shoot with several leaves.

Seeds can "play the field" in several ways. Wind plays a large role, as does wildlife such as woodpeckers and squirrels. Seeds can stick to feathers or fur, where they are carried off and eventually fall to the ground and take root. Seeds don't have to be small and windblown to survive, however. Coconuts are a palm tree's seed. They are buoyant and can float in the ocean for miles and miles before washing ashore on a beach and sprouting.

Reproduction is basically the same for the coniferous trees. Each year, a new set of cones opens on the tall pines. Like the needles, the little green cones are formed in the buds the year before and stand upright on the branches. On the female cone, there are scales that wind around it in a spiral. These scales open up parts of the cone just long enough to catch the pollen grains flying in the air from the male sperm cells. If the pollen grains hook up with a female egg cell inside the seeds of the cone, an embryo is formed.

Pollen that isn't fertilized doesn't disappear. Asthma sufferers can tell when trees are reproducing, as the non-fertilized pollen causes allergies, stuffy noses and other medical problems. Interestingly, of the 600-700 tree species native to North

America, only pollen from about 65 of these trees has been shown to cause allergies. But if you suffer from just one, it is quite enough!

Most coniferous seeds leave the parent tree in the fall but don't start growing until the spring. When the seeds are ready to grow, the cone scales change from green to light brown, hang upside down, dry out and then open. If the seed lands on fertile soil, it will become a little seedling pine. But not all seeds mature within one year.

The giant sequoia cones take at least two years to mature and may remain on the tree for up to 20 years. On average, one giant sequoia produces more than 1,500 cones a year. Given the hundreds of years (even thousands) most live, a mature tree may have up to 40,000 cones at any time. About one-third of them are dry and will never grow into trees.

The giant sequoia, along with several other conifers like the lodge pole pine, need fire in order to free their seeds. In a bizarre twist of Mother Nature, the trees require heat to dry out the cones high above the wildfire, thus releasing the seeds to the wind.

CHAPTER FOUR

FOREST TYPES

*"The clearest way into the universe
is through a forest wilderness."*
~ John Muir

The United States is a remarkable country. The diversity of our forests is one example. The four types of forests—boreal, temperate, subtropic and tropical—are classified according to their geographic distribution and location. Of course, under each class are a number of subcategories such as rain forests, montane forests, chaparrals, savannas and cloud forests. Every type of forest exists in the USA, and I hope this chapter will give you an idea not only of the great diversity of forests that exist here, but in other parts of the world as well. We need this diversity, and it's important to understand what these different types of forests can be used for, and what they need in order to remain healthy.

Right now, about 30 percent of the world's land is taken up by trees, 11 percent by cropland, 26 percent by ranges and pastures, and a little more than 33 percent by that very important category, "other"—meaning cities, towns and shopping malls. Percentage-wise, Latin America has the greatest amount of forest, about 22 percent of its territory, followed by North America and Russia with 19 percent each and Africa with 18 percent. Thirteen percent of Asia is covered in forests, and sadly, only four percent of Europe is forestland. Russia, Canada and the United States mostly have boreal coniferous or temperate deciduous forests. Africa has the largest amount of open woodlands.

There are four layers to a forest. The uppermost layer is the canopy, which can be as high as two hundred feet above the ground, especially in the tropical forests. The canopy forms the leafy part of the forest and absorbs about half of the sunlight. About four-fifths of the world's forests are "closed canopy" forests, meaning that the tree crowns spread over 20 percent or more of the ground, with potential for commercial purposes. The other one-fourth is open canopy forest or woodland.

Below the canopy are the middle layers, which consist of understory and shrub layers. The smaller trees and bushes live here. Some of these trees are just waiting for an opening in the canopy in order to catch the sunlight and grow to their full height. Also found in the understory are trees, bushes, grasses and legumes that grow best in shady conditions.

The ground cover includes the small plants that live on the ground, like ferns. The soil is the fourth layer of the forest, and it is full of activity and life. Found in the soil are bacteria, fungi and animals that do the important job of recycling dead plant and animal matter, turning it back into a form that can be used by the plants and trees.

TEMPERATE FORESTS

The temperate forests, also known as deciduous forests, are located almost entirely in the vast landmasses of the Northern Hemisphere. In the Southern Hemisphere, temperate forests generally grow only at the tips of the African and South American continents.

Over most of this zone, temperatures change from hot in the summer to cold in the winter. In this area, there is a five- to six-month growing season, with fertile soils due to plenty of leaf litter. On average, they receive about 30 to 60 inches of rain yearly, and it's evenly distributed throughout the year.

Deciduous forests once covered most of Europe and parts of Japan and Australia. It's hard to believe that most of the land around the Mediterranean Sea, including Spain, southern France and Greece, was covered with oak, pine, cedar and laurel forests. Due to land clearing for industrial and agricultural pur- poses, only fragments of those original forests remain, most of them now covered with maqui, a dense, scrubby growth.

In some parts of the world, including the U.S. and Canada, temperate forests can contain broadleaf as well as conifers. Actually, the forests in the southeastern U.S., including the trees on our Charlane Plantation, once were largely deciduous forests, but through the efforts of man, are now mainly coniferous forests. Areas that were once rich with beech, maple and oak, are now home to loblolly, slash, longleaf and shortleaf pines.

But the temperate forests still have an assorted list of trees, including birches, aspens, elm, ash, beech and maples. One reason for this diversity is that during the Ice Age, the glaciers never came that far south. Many species that died out farther north can still be found here.

However, trees in the temperate forests must still be able to survive cold winters. For pine trees, that is less of a problem because the shape and texture of their needles are designed to endure ice and subzero cold. But for the broadleaf trees, sur- vival requires desperate measures: the shedding of their energy- producing leaves before surrendering to an icy winter hiber- nation. Not unlike the grand, melodramatic soprano diva of a

Temperate seasonal forest, Northern California.

magnificent opera, the leaves give us their most glorious performance of their lives just before dying, turning from green
to grandiloquent shades of red, orange and yellow.

Because these forests are so diverse, I find them particularly
interesting. Take the forests in Colorado. Although the forests
there are mostly evergreen, Colorado has about three million
acres of aspens, which are a marvel of nature. Aspens are pioneer trees, meaning they're among the first to grow when the
land is cleared due to fire, storms or logging. They don't even
have to rely on seeds to reproduce—new trees can grow from
the roots of other trees. As many of us know, Colorado in the
fall is spectacular, due to the display of the aspens' brilliant
color. They're easy to spot among the evergreens.

Another temperate forest, but one distinctly different from
Colorado's, is the Smoky Mountains of Tennessee and North
Carolina. Not only is there a nice mix of hardwoods and evergreens, but about 25 percent of the half-million acres of the
Great Smoky Mountains National Park is old-growth forest. It
very well may be the best example of undisturbed hardwood
forest in the U.S., with more than 100 kinds of trees and
1,500 species of vascular plants. That, by the way, is more than
is found in all of northern Europe.

But my favorite forest is the Southern pine forest, like our
own Charlane Plantation. Our climate is warm—semi-tropi-
cal—and there are several soil types ranging from sandy and
sandy loam to black river bottoms and red clay. The famous
Georgia red clay stops around the fall line, actually near our
place. Because of these conditions, Southern forests are fast
growing. The South can produce high-quality saw timber pine
trees in 20 to 30 years.

The backbone of the Southern forest goes by many names:
Arkansas pine, black pine, North Carolina pine, old field pine,
and loblolly pine. Call it what you will, the loblolly pine can

grow over 100 feet tall and two to five feet in diameter. Loblolly needles are six to nine inches in length, whereas the needles of the longleaf pine, which look a little like the slash pine needles but longer, grow in length from nine to 18 inches. A medium-lived tree reaches full maturity in about 150 years, with select trees growing as old as 300 years or more.

In addition to their dozens of commercial uses, the loblolly, longleaf and slash pines play an important role in nature. White-tailed deer, gray squirrel, fox squirrel, bobwhite quail and wild turkey all use these trees for shelter. The red-cockaded woodpeckers use old-growth longleaf for nesting, and so do a variety of other bird species such as the pine warbler, brown-headed nuthatch and Bachman's warbler.

BOREAL FOREST

The boreal forest is also known as the coniferous forest or the taiga. The boreal forest is found in a broad band around the world between 45 degrees to 60 degrees northern latitude. This area gets about 12 to 40 inches of precipitation, much of which is snow. In the boreal rain forests, however, more than 150 inches of rain could fall annually.

In the boreal forests, conifers—such as spruce, larch and fir—are the primary trees because they can thrive in areas with poor, sandy soil, low precipitation and a short growing season. To compensate for tough conditions, they develop thin, spiny, needlelike evergreen leaves with a thick waxy coat. These needles don't require as much water as the broadleaf trees; nor do they shed their leaves. With the exception of the tamarack and a few other species, most conifers keep their needles not only through the winter season but for years. Most conifers have the same needles for two to three years, and a spruce can hold on to the same needle for 15 years.

A red-cockaded woodpecker working on a longleaf pine.

A boreal forest in the Pacific Northwest.

UNIV. OF GEORGIA SCHOOL OF FORESTRY

In the upper regions of the boreal forest, south of the Arctic Circle, is a forest subset called the taiga. Parts of Canada, Russia, Scandinavia and Alaska have taiga forests. Although this is the land of moose, caribou, wolves and black bears, the forest contains mainly dwarf birch and labrador tea trees. In fact, the Athapaskan Indians, who roamed Alaska, called the taiga the "land of little sticks."

Although some classify the Pacific Northwest and California areas as temperate rain forests, I view them more as boreal forests. I've visited these areas many times and am rejuvenated and inspired each time I go. On the "Bridges to Babylon" tour, I took my younger daughter Ashley with me to walk the famous Muir Woods, just north of San Francisco. If you haven't been there, it should be on your list of places to visit, as I promise it won't disappoint!

Before the settlers and loggers came, there were about 31 million acres of virgin forest in the Pacific Northwest. Less than 15 percent remains today. British Columbia has felled at least 60 percent of the richest and most productive old-growth forests.

These forests are home to the marbled murrelet, wonderfully colorful flowers like the Indian paintbrush, lupine and white daises, and the northern spotted owl. In the 1970s, scientists said that only about 200 pairs of the northern spotted owls existed, and there was a loud fight between loggers and environmentalists over protecting the birds. Today, there are more than 3,600 pairs.

In terms of trees, this area boasts redwoods, western red cedars, Douglas firs, hemlocks and Sitka spruces. These are just magnificent trees. Redwoods, for example, can grow as tall as 350 feet or more. The largest ever recorded, at 367.8 feet, was discovered in 1963 by a National Geographic Society team. Although not the tallest, the Dyerville Giant Redwood is the thickest, with its trunk measuring more than 52 feet in circumference. The redwoods flourish in a 500-mile long fog belt that goes just south to the Monterey Peninsula to just north of the Oregon border.

Another wonder is the giant sequoia tree that grows naturally in about 75 groves on the Sierra's western slopes, mainly in elevations of 5,000 to 7,000 feet. In terms of family, the sequoias are cousins of the coastal redwoods of California and the dawn redwoods of central China.

It is in the Giant Forest, so named by naturalist John Muir, where the General Sherman Tree can be found. The General Sherman Tree is the largest living organism on this earth – plant or animal. At 275 feet tall, with a circumference of 103 feet and diameter of 36 feet at the base, the volume of the Sherman Tree was calculated to be slightly over 52,500 cubic feet.

The world's oldest living tree is the bristlecone pine, found in the White Mountains, just east of the Sierra Nevada

Mountains in eastern California. The growth rings of several of these trees have shown that they live more than 4,000 years. One tree, dubbed Methuselah, discovered in 1958, is today 4,769 years old.

What's intriguing about the bristlecone pine is that it is not a tall or stately tree. In fact, it is very slow-growing—about one inch in diameter every 100 years—and up to 25 to 30 feet tall. Up to 90 percent of the tree may be dead wood, but it is surrounded and protected by a thin vein of living tissue. Only one other type of tree—the limber pine—survives in these mountains. But the bristlecone pines have lived for centuries quite oblivious to the harsh conditions. In fact, the tree can adjust to almost impossible conditions—even stopping its growth—sort of a tree's version of a bear's hibernation.

SUBTROPICAL FORESTS

The line between a tropical and subtropical forest isn't great. A subtropical forest is outside of the equatorial zone, meaning it's more around the Tropics of Cancer and Capricorn than the equator. One difference between a tropical and a subtropical forest is that the subtropical forest has the hot, humid temperatures of a tropical forest, but it has a dry season as well. Subtropical forests can be found in southeastern South America, coastal southeast South Africa, eastern Australia and eastern Asia from northern India through south China to Japan. Hawaii and the southernmost tip of Florida have the only subtropical forests in this country.

Some scientists believe that classifying the two forests by climate is too simple, preferring to classify rain forests on the basis of the leaf size of canopy trees and the complexity of the forest's structure. Since I'm not a scientist, we'll leave that debate alone.

Subtropical forest, Puerto Rico.

YALE UNIV. SCHOOL OF FORESTRY

These areas have incredibly diverse native plants, animals, birds and coral reefs. For instance, in the 130-acre forest area in Lambir, Malaysia, there are 1,200 tree species. By comparison, there are only about 700 tree species in the entire U.S. and Canada.

Hawaii is a good example of an area with subtropical forests. In Hawaii's forests can be found the Ala'a, sandalwood, the Honduras mahogany and the kassod tree. The baobab tree, native to Africa, is also found in Hawaii. Its nickname is "the dead rat tree" because its seedpods resemble rats hanging by their tails from its branches.

TROPICAL FORESTS

Tropical forests, often called jungles, can be found in some regions of South and Central America, Africa, Southeast Asia and some of the Pacific Islands that are within 23 degrees latitude of the equator. There are several subsets of tropical forests, but all have substantial rainfall and uniform temperature. Collectively, they cover roughly 8 percent of the earth's land surface—about the size of the U.S.

Tropical forests get lots of rain, usually between 60 to 120 inches a year, in some places as much as 300 inches a year. Temperatures are warm to hot year-round, rarely going below 80 degrees, with the area getting about 12 hours of sun a day.

The soil tends to be thin, acidic and nutrient-poor, though hundreds of tree species don't seem to mind. In fact, the forest acts as a sponge and soaks up the moisture in the vegetation and, through the tree roots, releases it back into the atmosphere. Actually, the growth in the tropical forests depends not on food from the soil, but on the rapid decomposition and recycling of dead organic matter. In fact, the soil is so poor and the ground so moist, it would be easy for the trees to fall down. Mother Nature to the rescue: Trees in the rain forests have buttresses, which are only found here.

Buttresses are like outspread wings from the bottom of a tree trunk that help brace it up. Support also comes from lianas, the thick, cable-like vines that grow everywhere and weave their way through the forest canopy, helping to hold the trees in a big net. Sometimes these lianas can be as thick as a man's thigh and are so strong that trees can even bend and break off from their roots—and still not fall.

Rain forests are a cornucopia of tree species. One single rain forest in Peru contains more than 300 different tree species. Even more amazing is the number of plants, like orchids, that are found growing *in* these trees. So far, more than 25,000 species of orchids have been identified and there's still more to count.

It's so dense in the jungle that all its species live incredibly close together. Birds and mammals live in the top of the canopy and feed on leaves, fruit, nectar and insects. Flying bats and mammals live in the middle canopy and feed mainly on insects. On the ground are large herbivores and carnivores, such as gorillas, as well as countless smaller animal species. Throughout the whole are insects, the number of species estimated to be in the millions.

Tropical forests, thought to contain more than two-thirds of all plant biomass and at least half of the animal, plant and microbial species in the world, now occupy less than 10 percent of the earth's surface. At the beginning of this century, an estimated 12.5 million square kilometers of tropic lands were covered with closed canopy forest— that's larger than the U.S. Today a little less than 1 percent of the remaining tropical forest is cleared each year. That's not good. The extinction of species due to this clearing is shameful. I know that some will argue the economics of clearing the forest, but there are other ways for the people of these forests to improve their lifestyles without destroying the forests.

The crisis of the diminishing rain forests has been well publicized, thanks in part to my fellow musicians and entertainers, particularly Sting, who have taken up the cause. They're right. We need to pay attention. Some rain forests are in trouble.

The rain forests of Brazil contain an awesome inventory of life. Although Brazil has the largest tropical forest area—some 3 million square miles, it also has one of the highest rates of deforestation in the world.

The 7,000-acre Guai Acu Reserve in Brazil has more than 430 species of birds. Of those 430 species, 120 are totally dependent on the forest for their survival. Fifty species are listed as threatened or near threatened. This area is also one of the last havens for the woolly spider monkey, which is one of the world's rarest primates with only 400 living.

Moist tropical forest, Papua New Guinea.

Other areas have lost a great proportion of their forests. The coastal forests of Ecuador, Sierra Leone, Ghana, Madagascar, Cameron, and Liberia have mostly been destroyed. Haiti was once 80 percent forestland; now its forest is mostly gone.

Another threatened rain forest is closer to home. The Caribbean National Forest in Puerto Rico is the only tropical rain forest among the national forests in the U.S. An area of only 28,000 acres, this forest has a variety of uses, including recreation. It also is home to one of the world's most endangered species, the Puerto Rican parrot. Fewer than 40 are known to be living in the forest, which is especially heartbreaking because not too long ago more than one million of these colorful birds graced the island.

A common misconception is that all parts of a rain forest are alike. The rain forest in Puerto Rico is a good example of why that isn't true. The lowest level, the tabonuco forest, is below 2,000 feet and is named for the straight and tall tabonuco trees, which are among the 225 native tree species there. In fact, 23 species grow there and nowhere else.

The next zone, the palo colorado forest, is the home of the endangered parrot, which nests in cavities of the palo colorado trees. The third zone, the sierra palm forest, has much steeper terrain, while the final zone, the dwarf or cloud forest, is above 2,500 feet. The highest zone is characterized by trees with stunted growth. Two species found nowhere else in the world call this zone home: the Burrow coqui, a frog, and the Elfin Woods Warbler, which wasn't even discovered until 1971!

Another important rain forest is in Danjugan, an island in the Philippines. It is one of the few islands in that country which still has its original tropical forests. A stopping-off place for migratory birds like swallows, waders and kingfishers, this forest is teeming with wildlife, including bats, birds and turtles. Both of its turtle species—the green turtle and the hawksbill turtle—are endangered.

The rain forests of Belize overflow with howler monkeys, spider monkeys, tapirs, jaguars, ocelots, margays and more than 500 species of birds. More than 250 types of orchids bless this land, and the insect life is so abundant that many species have yet to be identified.

Another type of tropical forest is the tropical seasonal forest that exists in areas of India, Southeast Asia, Australia, West Africa, the West Indies and South America. While the rain forest has rain all the time, the tropical seasonal forests have definite wet and dry seasons. The wet period is often called the Monsoon season. These seasonal forests boast semi-evergreen or partly deciduous forests but also have open woodlands and grassy savannas.

Whenever I travel, I try to visit forests—either on an individual's private land, land owned by a timber company, or simply an area park or national forest. It's always interesting, and I recommend that when you travel anywhere—or even around your own town—go into the local woods and try to identify some of the trees or animals you see. It helps give you a better understanding of your place on earth when you see all the other living creatures in their proper place as well.

CHAPTER FIVE

AMERICAN FORESTS, A BRIEF HISTORY

*"To exist as a Nation, to prosper as a State,
and to live as a people, we must have trees."*
~ Theodore Roosevelt

What did the Indians and the European settlers see when they first landed? It wasn't amber waves of grain . . . it was trees.

In a very real sense, the history of our country is the history of our forests. Perhaps the single most significant event in the evolution of the modern American landscape was the clearing of forests for agriculture, fuel and building material. As we moved west, millions of trees were cut down to make room.

We weren't always kind to the land after we cleared it. The trees were so plentiful they were taken for granted—in some cases until it was too late. But the truth is that our forefathers and mothers were absolutely dependent upon the products of the forest, both in their personal lives and in the general economy. It was a blessing and a curse that we had so much.

The original forest, including Alaska, covered about one billion acres. That's about half of our country. About three-quarters of the forest was in the eastern part of the country. Believe it or not, about 70 percent of that original forest still exists.

COLONISTS AND THE FOREST

When the first English settlers, led by Sir Walter Raleigh, landed at Roanoke Island, Virginia, in 1585, they were greeted by the Roanoke Indians and a thick covering of trees: American holly, bald cypress, black cherry, dwarf sumac, hickory, redbud, spruce pine and sycamore, among others. In fact, Captain Arthur Barlowe, one of the explorers, wrote that they found Roanoke Island to be a "most pleasant and fertile ground, replenished with goodly Cedars, and divers other sweet woods."

In 1586, another small band of settlers came, including some women and children, but by 1587, the famous "Lost Colony" had disappeared. While there are a few theories as to what happened, no one knows for sure. The only trace of the Lost Colony exists in one of those trees, where someone carved the word "Croatan" into the bark. To this day, nobody knows who carved it or what it means.

The next group of settlers—the first permanent European settlers—landed nearby in Jamestown, Virginia, in 1602. They met the Algonquian Indians, including Pocahontas.

Captain John Smith and his fellow colonists would have spotted the black or wild cherry, which is a medium-size tree that seldom grows more than 50 feet tall, with wide, spreading branches. They would have also seen the black walnut tree, which grows to more than 100 feet. While this stately tree was prevalent during the colonial period, only a few specimens remain in the Virginia area today.

Both the Indians and early colonists used the bark, twigs and roots of the ancient sassafras tree for medicinal purposes. The red-brown bark was boiled and used as a permanent orange dye for clothes. The sassafras, which seldom grows higher than 40 feet, is a tree of amazing lineage. Fossil leaves have been found embedded in the rock strata of our western mountains as well as in European formations

In 1620, the Pilgrims landed at Plymouth Rock, Massachusetts, where pine and oak foliage would have provided a bright mosaic of mixed forests. Other early settlers found a deciduous and coniferous forest in New England, pine trees down the southern coastal plain and Piedmont, and a variety of hardwoods in the central and southern Appalachians through the Ohio Valley and into the Midwest. Pine and oak predominated in Texas, Missouri, Indiana, Illinois and Ohio. The Pacific area boasted pine, redwood, Douglas fir, spruce and hemlock.

The American chestnut was plentiful during this time, thriving in most of the eastern half of the U.S. from Maine to Minnesota and south to Florida and Mississippi. The tree was valued for its high quality wood and delicious nuts. Unfortunately, a fungus disease, introduced into this country around 1900, killed most of the American chestnut trees on the eastern seaboard in less than 25 years. Scientists and horticulturists are still trying to find a way to save and grow this tree.

An unusual tree that had camellia-like, single white flowers and deep green leaves was another familiar sight in the Southeast. John Bartram, appointed by King George III to be a botanist for the "Colonies," and his son William discovered the tree and named it Franklinia for Benjamin Franklin. Impressed by its beauty, they fortunately sent some seeds and plants to the Bartram garden in Pennsylvania around 1765. Three hundred years later, there are Franklinia trees all over this country in gardens—and every one of them comes directly from the seeds and plants saved by the Bartrams.

America's first settlers found thousands of plant and animal species, a land of unbelievable life, diversity and richness. Even in the 1700s, the woodlands were basically untouched, except

Gigantic American chestnut trees used to be plentiful.

for some small clearings made by the native Americans and pioneers. Of course, the Native Americans knew how to live off the land and taught that valuable lesson to the settlers. Living off the land meant understanding the forest and knowing how to cultivate all of its riches.

Indians cleared trees to plant crops, and in what may be the first example of forest management, even practiced controlled burning, something we still do today. The Indians knew that a seasonal burn would improve game habitat, reduce insect pests, remove cover from potential enemies and generally help the land. Virginia's beautiful Shenandoah Valley was once vast grass prairie due to annual burns set by native people. Fire-created openings grew grasses and forbs bountiful enough to support populations of bison in the early 1600s on the East Coast.

The Pilgrims learned their lessons well from the Native Americans, but they quickly saw the economic value of trees. Lumber was one of the country's first exports. Only a year after the Mayflower landed at Plymouth Rock, the colonists were sending clapboard back to the Old World. England's forests already had been largely destroyed, and early settlers soon became a main source for ship masts and timbers. In return, they received vital dry goods and materials from England.

However, though the forests provided a great wealth of resources to the settlers, the trees were in the way of land they wanted to conquer, own and farm. Settlers soon were busy clearing forests to build houses, barns, bridges, dams and other buildings. In order to keep the farm animals from wandering, fences were necessary—a tremendous ordeal both in terms of manpower and trees. A square 40-acre field enclosed by a zigzag fence needed about 8,000 fence rails to do the job. The average farmer could split 50 to 100 rails a day. The fence-making continued at an incredible pace, and by 1850, there were about 3.2 million miles of wooden fences in the U.S.—enough to circle the globe 120 times.

Unfortunately, demand soon overtook what seemed to be an endless supply. Forests became depleted, and with the loss of the trees, wildlife that the people counted on for food and furs moved on or died. By the mid 1700s game animals such as deer, eastern elk, wild turkey and beaver were becoming scarce in some areas.

Gifford Pinchot, one of our country's first forest managers, wrote that land's value was neither understood nor prized. "Get timber by hook or by crook, get it quick and cut it quick—that was the rule of the citizen," he wrote. "And it has been got rid of both by the government and the private owners with amazing efficiency and startling speed. Maine and Pennsylvania had sold great areas for a shilling an acre, and North Carolina, for ten cents an acre, had disposed of some of the finest hardwood stands in the East. The richest government timberlands could be bought for $2.50 an acre."

Wood was not only used to build houses, it warmed them as well. An average household easily would burn 20 to 40 cords annually. A cord of wood weighs about two tons and has the heating value of a ton of coal or 200 gallons of fuel oil. In the late 1700s, about two-thirds of the volume of wood cut from the forests was used for energy. It wasn't uncommon to burn more wood in one year for heating and cooking than was used to build the house being heated.

Wood was used to cook food, produce the iron in the industrial mills, and drive the locomotive trains, steamboats and stationary engines. Just about everything our forefathers did, made, ate or used, involved wood.

When you consider that the U.S. population from 1785 to 1850 grew from three million people to 23.3 million, it's clear that the forests were being used up at an alarming rate. The volume of wood used in 1850 (a little after a young Abe Lincoln was splitting rails), was six times the volume at the beginning of that century.

If we were to revert back to this way of life, Americans would use 1.6 billion cords of wood each year just to heat our homes. It would take two billion acres of productive forest devoted solely to firewood production to meet this end.

WESTWARD HO! AND MORE TREES MUST GO!

As the Industrial Revolution made its way through the U.S., colorful steamboats were used to transport goods down our rivers to new cities—inspiring writers like Mark Twain and the musicians who created a sound called Dixieland. Of course, steamboats ran on wood (to heat the fire to make the steam) and were made of wood. In 1840, almost 90,000 cords of wood were sold for steamboat fuel—about one-fifth of all fuel wood sold.

As we know, our rivers alone couldn't dictate the country's growth. Horace Greeley said, "Go West, young man," and the young men did, driving wooden covered wagons in perilous journeys across the country—too perilous and too slow.

Mid-century brought the advent of a better form of transportation. The first railroad built here was only three miles in length, extending from the granite quarries of Quincy, Massachusetts, to the Noponset River. But between 1850 to 1920, the number of miles of U.S. railroads increased from less than 100,000 miles to more than 350,000. By the late 1800s, railroads accounted for almost a quarter of the country's consumption of timber.

In 1862, Congress passed the first of several Railroad Acts, mandating a rail route that went from Omaha, Nebraska, to Sacramento, California—much of it an old pioneer trail. Two companies were responsible for building the railroad – the

Crossties by the thousands.

FOREST HISTORY SOCIETY

Central Pacific, which started in the West, and the Union Pacific from the East.

When we think of the railroads, the popular, romantic vision is of a hearty steel train chugging its way across the land, vulnerable to attacks by Indians and outlaws, weather and mechanical breakdowns. The less-than-romantic reality was that more than 20,000 men working from both sides of the country sacrificed years of their lives putting down the wood crossties and steel rails on top and driving steel spikes to hold them down. Each mile of track required more than 2,500 cross ties. The final spike was driven into the tie at Promontory Summit, Utah, in 1869.

It's ironic that the early railroads were called "iron horses," because far more wood was used than iron. Except for the

FOREST HISTORY SOCIETY

Trestles like this one used vast amounts of timber.

engine, rails, steel wheels and frames, it was all wood: the cars, crossties, fuel, the bridges and trestles, station houses, fences and telegraph poles.

Since wood was not treated with preservatives until the beginning of this century, all the crossties had to be replaced every five to seven years. Considering the miles of track that existed in 1910, the crossties on more than 50,000 miles of track were being replaced each year. Fifteen to 20 million acres of forests were used to provide wood just for cross ties in 1900.

Just as highways do today, the railroad further opened the country up to development. To keep up with the population growth, more forests had to be cleared for agricultural purposes. Between 1850 and 1910, more than 190 million acres of forests were cleared to make way for crops and pasture—an amount bigger than the total of the entire previous 250 years. During these years, farmers cleared more than 13.5 square miles of forests daily. Over this 60-year period, more than 23 percent of the forests in the Pacific Coast and Southwest—44 million acres—went under the plow. Even more staggering is that 76 percent of all forests in the East and South was cleared during this time.

Ohio is a good example. In 1800, 96 percent of the state was covered in hardwood forests. Fifty years later, it was 60 percent, but by 1900 only 25 percent of the state was forested. Almost 75 percent of the forests had been destroyed in just one hundred years.

Wildfire added to the destruction of the forests around the turn of the century. By 1900, between 20 to 50 million acres of forests were lost annually to these types of fires. To get an idea of what we're talking about, that's the size of Virginia, West Virginia, Maryland and Delaware combined. As a result, More than 80 million acres of land remained idle or lacked desirable trees, thanks to bad—meaning nonexistent—land practices.

Of course, the disappearance of the U.S. forests dramatically affected the country's wildlife. Several abundant species, such as the white-tailed deer, wild turkey, longhorn moose, black bear, bighorn sheep and bison, were severely depleted. Beavers were eliminated from much of their homeland. By the early 1900s, the passenger pigeon, one of the most abundant birds on the continent, was nearly extinct, as was an eastern relative of the western prairie chicken. Gone forever is the great auk, a flightless bird once found on the northeast coast.

STOP THE DESTRUCTION

As early as 1865, Frederic Star foresaw a "national famine of wood." The vast destruction could no longer be overlooked.

Fortunately, as is often the case in times of trouble, visionary men who had great passion for the forests rose to the occasion. In a later chapter, we'll introduce such men as John Muir, Gifford Pinchot, George Perkins Marsh, Theodore Roosevelt and others who stopped the insanity surrounding our use of the forests.

As these revolutionary men took up the good fight for the forests, it also happened that timber consumption took a dive. After 1910, fossil fuels replaced wood fuels, and steel and concrete became the standard building materials. The country turned to coal and oil for its energy needs. Although the volume of wood used in the early 1900s for energy remained high, it met a progressively lower proportion of U.S. energy needs. (Today only about 3 percent of U.S. energy resources come from wood.)

By 1905 per capita consumption rates for wood were more than 500 board feet per year. By 1970, that figure plunged to 200 board feet. By the 1920s the wholesale clearing of forestland had abated. The clearing that still took place was offset by farmland abandonment (remember the Dust Bowl and the Great Depression). In many areas, the land reverted back to its natural forest state. This was also the time that the conservation movement took hold, and vast areas were saved for national forests. By the 1940s, national wood consumption was 15 percent lower than at the start of the century.

If the Industrial Revolution and railroads were responsible for bringing people to all parts of the country who then cut down the trees, technology played a role in stabilizing cropland and reducing the need to clear more forests. For a start, mules weren't needed once tractors came into wide use. In 1910, it took 27 percent of all cropland just to keep and raise the food for the mules. By 1950, about 70 million acres of that land could be used instead for human consumption.

Furthermore, our methods of farming, including fertilizers and genetically improved hybrid crops, dramatically improved the land's productivity. Today's American farmers grow at least five times the crop yield per acre they did in 1920. More crops on less land is a winning combination.

IT'S GETTING BETTER ALL THE TIME

Today we have many forces in play to ensure that our woods are not wasted. We have a more efficient way to saw the lumber, and almost nothing is wasted. In addition, engineering standards and designs have reduced the amount of wood needed to build a house or building. Vast amounts of time, money and effort go into making our use of wood as efficient as possible, which reduces the number of trees that must be cut down.

Recycling also helps. Each year, paper is used to publish more than two million books, 350 million magazines and 245 billion newspapers in this country, which means that the average American today uses 686 pounds of paper. Fortunately, about 48 percent of all paper is recovered for reuse.

Our national park system has also saved millions of acres from destruction. We now have 106 million acres in the federal wilderness system and another 153 million in parks, wildlife refuges and other special set-aside places. We should all be very proud of this. No other country in the world comes close to this amount of legally designated set-aside land.

As the Beatles sang in their classic "Hey Jude," we've taken a sad song and made it better. While scientists differ on the definition of an old-growth forest, today there are more than 14.8 million acres of "late successional" and other reserved forest habitat in the Pacific Northwest. Each year more than 1.6 billion seedlings are planted. That's five new trees a year for every American.

Tree farmers are practicing better land management, protecting the overall environment as well as ensuring enough forests for future generations. In Georgia, for instance, we have replanted more than three billion trees over the past decade.

Today the annual growth of commercial forests exceeds both the harvest and losses to insects, fire and disease by about 49 percent annually.

Not only are the forests more vital than they have been for decades, but the wildlife is making a comeback as well. The white-tailed deer population has grown from 4.5 million to more than 16 million in the past 30 years. Wild turkeys, once almost extinct, now number about four million today. In the early 1970s, there were only 200 pairs of northern spotted owls. Today, as noted earlier, there are approximately 3,600. Other species under protection, such as the red-cockaded woodpecker, are making a comeback due to conservation efforts of concerned parties, including those that work in the forest.

Our country's amazing story of how we came from so many places and formed this great land could not have been written without our vast forest resources: Trees fueled—literally and figuratively—our ability to expand and develop this country.

The story of America as an emerging nation was one of reckless waste and abuse of our trees. The story of today and the future is how we are conserving, properly managing, and in some cases protecting and still using our forests and trees. We have finally learned how to be good stewards of our forests, to ensure that there will be enough forest resources to continue for generations to come.

CHAPTER SIX

⌒

PIONEERS OF THE AMERICAN FORESTS

"Never doubt that a small group of thoughtful,
committed citizens can change the world.
Indeed, it's the only thing that ever has."
- Margaret Mead

It's a fascinating cosmic coincidence that throughout history the right people seem to come along at just the right time to effect major change.

Think of the minds that wrote the Declaration of Independence and the Constitution—including Jefferson, Monroe, Washington, Adams, Hamilton, Franklin and Madison. In a country with a population equivalent to that of a small city today, they all suddenly appeared to help invent a new form of government and show that people can rule themselves successfully with liberty and justice for all.

And in the area of music, just when the American genre (perhaps reflecting the mass production mentality of the fifties) became trite, boring, and mechanistic, in came the Beatles and the Rolling Stones to shake up our thinking, our dancing and our lives. They mobilized the enthusiasm, imagination and restlessness of our youth, inspiring them to help make pivotal changes in the role of women, blacks and youth in our culture. Not to mention the peace process and the environmental movement.

And so it was with forests. A series of men, some in power, some not, some quite literate, others, like Johnny Appleseed, perhaps unable to read, each in his own way started the shift in our collective thinking that our forests were a boundless resource to use, discard and disregard. Instead they offered the revelation that forests and nature would be lost if not taken care of, and therefore, a change in the way we treated our resources and the environment was necessary. Their influence resonates today as the ideological differences between nature protection and managed use continue to spark debate.

The concept of large-scale natural preservation for public enjoyment was not something that most people in the 1800s thought about or even considered. But an artist, George Catlin, did. Best known for his paintings of Native Americans, he started worrying about the destructive effects of the country's westward expansion on Indian civilization, wildlife and wilderness. After a trip to North and South Dakota in 1832, he wrote that the wilderness could be preserved by "some great protecting policy of government ... in a magnificent park ... a nation's park, containing man and beast, in all the wild[ness] and freshness of their nature's beauty."

Of course, no one paid much attention.

Gifford Pinchot, America's first professional forester, said that those who supported the forests were thought of as "impractical theorists, fanatics, or 'denudatics' more or less touched in the head. What talk there was about forest protection was no more to the average American than the buzzing of a mosquito, and just as irritating."

But romantic portrayals of nature by writers like James Fenimore Cooper and Henry David Thoreau, and painters like Thomas Cole and Frederick Edwin Church, slowly took hold of the country's imagination.

Abraham Lincoln, who certainly traveled his own enlightened path, saw the need to preserve the land. Even as the Civil War raged, Lincoln in 1864 transferred the Yosemite Valley and nearby Mariposa Big Tree Grove from federal ownership to the state of California on the condition that the lands would "be held for public use, resort and recreation ... inalienable for all time."

Despite plenty of opposition, in 1872 President Ulysses S. Grant signed the Yellowstone Act, which allowed more than two million acres to be "dedicated and set apart as a public park or . . . for the benefit and enjoyment of the people." From then on, Yellowstone National Park would be under the control of the Secretary of the Interior, who was to "provide for the preservation, from injury or spoliation, of all timber, mineral deposits, natural curiosities, or wonders within said park, and their retention in their natural condition."

Soon afterwards, most of Mackinac Island in Michigan was turned into a national park under the U.S. Army, which had a fort on the island. In 1895, Congress transferred the federal lands to Michigan for a state park.

The next generation of great scenic national parks, including Sequoia and Yosemite, came in 1890 and were created by President Benjamin Harrison.

All of these parks were largely preserved for their aesthetic qualities. Basically, Congress said the lands weren't good for anything else but to be pretty—it was no great loss to just set them aside. Congress controlled the parks and frequently had to be assured that the lands in question were worthless for other purposes, such as timber, farming or development.

Not everyone bought into the theory that beautiful land had no other purpose.

Gifford Pinchot believed that the forests could be preserved but only if managed properly—meaning that their economic value be realized.

Pinchot was born in 1876 to great wealth and was very much a part of the Progressive era. His studies in Europe introduced him to the theory that if you exploit natural resources you can actually save them. He believed that the greatest good could be achieved by scientifically and intensively managing resources, such as forests, for product use, so as to guarantee their continued productivity for generations.

Or, as Pinchot said, "Conservation is the application of common sense to the common problems for the common good." He wrote a primer about forestry entitled *The Practice of Forestry* (1903), and to better understand his philosophy, it's worth printing the introduction here:

"The Service of the Forest"

Next to the earth itself the forest is the most useful servant of man. Not only does it sustain and regulate the streams, moderate the winds, and beautify the land, but it also supplies wood, the most widely used of all materials. Its uses are numberless, and the demands that are made upon it by mankind are numberless also. It is essential to the well-being of mankind that these demands should be met. They must be met steadily, fully, and at the right time if the forest is to give its best service. The object of practical forestry is precisely to make the forest render its best service to man in such a way as to increase rather than to diminish its usefulness in the future. Forest management and conservative lumbering are other names for practical forestry. Under whatever name it may be known, practical forestry means both the use and the preservation of the forest.

Pinchot's views were spurred by a very real fear that the country would run out of trees as a result of its endless and unrestrained obsession for development. He also understood that forests were universes of animals and plants all dependent on each other for survival. It was his quest to bring all these needs together so they could be managed properly and profitably. What he needed was a place to put his ideas into action.

That place was soon provided by George Vanderbilt, who was building a beautiful and elaborate country estate near Asheville, North Carolina. At more than 7,000 acres, the Biltmore Estate included a model farm, a great arboretum, a vast game preserve and a forest that was to be run like a farm. Vanderbilt had heard of Pinchot through Frederick Law Olmsted, the famous landscape architect, whom he had hired to design the estate's gardens.

Thus the Biltmore Estate was the first woodland in the U.S. to be put under a regular system of forest management. Pinchot's objective was to give Vanderbilt a return on his investment and—just as importantly—actually improve the forest.

Pinchot's first step was to mark the forest—consisting of mostly oaks and other broadleafs along with some pines—with a topographical survey. After familiarizing himself with the land and the types of trees, Pinchot locked horns with the way the estate had been up until then managing the timber. Rather than cut out the young growth that would interfere with cheap and easy logging, he instructed that large trees surrounded by a dense growth of smaller trees be cut. In addition, he proved that the expense of being careful not to injure other trees was relatively minor. Finally, for every tree cut down, Pinchot planted four or five more.

Pinchot's hard work and theories paid off—literally and figuratively. The result was a lush and productive forest that in its first year made a grand profit of $1,220.56.

As Pinchot would eventually be called away from the Biltmore project for higher purpose, he brought in a fellow named Carl Schenck to carry on his work there. Schenck realized he needed trained men to help him, and started instructing the locals in forest management, thus establishing the first school of forestry in America.

After his work for Vanderbilt, Pinchot was in great demand as a consultant and eventually became involved with national policy. From 1898 to 1910, he served as chief of the Division of Forestry, in the Department of Agriculture, which eventually became the U.S. Forest Service. He served under three presidents—William McKinley, Theodore Roosevelt and William Howard Taft.

In 1905, Roosevelt transferred the forest reserves to the Department of Agriculture. An avid outdoorsman, Roosevelt was of a similar mind with Pinchot about "wise use" of the land. In 1901 he said, "The fundamental idea of forestry is the perpetuation of forests by use. Forest protection is not an end in itself; it is a means to increase and sustain the resources of our country and the industries which depended upon them. The preservation of our forests is an imperative business necessity."

Under Pinchot and Roosevelt's direction, rights were given to build dams to irrigate land, ranchers were granted grazing rights, forest companies got lumbering rights and minerals rights were sold. The department's forest officers maintained close control over what was happening to the land. Before trees could be cut, government forest officers had to be assured that another growth of timber would replace the ones being removed and that the water supply would not suffer. They had to be convinced that the timber was really needed. In addition, they kept a close eye on forest fires and fought them with the best tools available, primitive though they were.

Gifford Pinchot

When Roosevelt left office in 1909, more than 234 million acres had been set aside as forest reserves.

If Pinchot believed in using the forests for the common good, on the opposite side of the argument was John Muir, who believed that the forest's spiritual value was as important as any economic gain.

Born in 1838 in Scotland, Muir is perhaps our country's most famous and influential naturalist and conservationist. A wilderness explorer, he is renowned for his excursions in California's Sierra Nevada and in Alaska. In 1867, Muir was temporarily blinded following an injury at a carriage parts shop. After regaining his sight a month later, he developed a wanderlust to see everything he could. He decided to walk from Indianapolis to the Gulf of Mexico, which is about a thousand miles, and afterwards sailed to Cuba and Panama to pursue his newfound enthusiasm.

Perhaps no one else delighted in nature as much as John Muir. In 1912, he wrote, "Everybody needs beauty as well as bread, places to play in and pray in, where nature may heal and give strength to body and soul alike. Keep close to Nature's heart . . . and break clear away, once in a while, and climb a mountain or spend a week in the woods. Wash your spirit clean."

In his travels, he talked with mill workers, farmers and mountain folks. He concluded that the best land, as well as the water sources in the high mountains, had already be preempted by rich speculators, mill companies and public utility corporations. In the belief that farmers were forced to pay dearly for water, he gained a firsthand knowledge of land-and-water monopolies and vowed to fight them.

In 1938 he wrote, "The clearest way into the Universe is through a forest wilderness." As he explored our land, Muir took to writing in order to get readers—particularly Eastern intellectuals and government types—caught up in the wonders of nature. By 1875 he was intent on making the wilderness better known and loved. If people understood the intrinsic benefits of the forests, he reasoned, then people would protect them.

Muir didn't buy into Pinchot's pragmatic forest management ideas. In his eyes, they resulted in forest destruction, like floods, droughts and river channels filled with silt. He saw waste and destruction because of sawmills, fires set by men, and sheep that invaded the Sierra and destroyed grass.

In 1881, Muir tried to have more land set aside for Yosemite Valley and Mariposa Big Tree Grove, as well as for a public park in California. Though his efforts failed, he learned to a degree the art of politics and how to get bills passed in Washington, knowledge that came in handy when in 1890, he

Theodore Roosevelt, third from left, and John Muir, fifth from left.

again tried to have more land at Yosemite saved. This time he rallied the public, urging that letters, telegrams and petitions be sent to Congress, and his grassroots efforts worked.

Muir's ability to rally a collection of conservationists led to the founding in 1892 of the Sierra Club, today the most influential environmental group in the country. The Sierra Club's purpose is to "explore, enjoy and render accessible the mountain regions of the Pacific Coast; to publish authentic information concerning them; to enlist the support and cooperation of the people and government in preserving the forest and other natural features of the Sierra Nevada Mountains."

Muir traveled and wrote about the majestic beauty he saw. His works were published in popular magazines rather than stuffy scientific journals. As the public gobbled up Muir's words, he quickly politicized his growing following. In 1892 he fought a bill that proposed to cut Yosemite National Park in half and sell the lucrative timberland. It took three years, but Muir and the Sierra Club won.

It's not hard to see that Pinchot and Muir were on opposite ends of forest-use theories. Pinchot was strictly utilitarian with a commercial bent while Muir was an aesthetic-spiritualist believer. In 1898 in an article for *Atlantic Monthly*, Muir boldly attacked Pinchot's utilitarian concept of conservation. As a result, Muir became viewed as the authentic voice for preservation.

The two former friends came to nasty verbal blows several times, first over the harmfulness of sheep grazing, and later over the damming of the Hetch-Hetchy Valley in California in order to provide water to San Francisco. The debate over the damming continued long after their deaths; as recently as 1997, Nevada ranchers and the U.S. Forest Service were locking horns over claims of vested watering rights. Pinchot's words were used during the trial.

While Muir and Pinchot perhaps are the bookends of the conservation movement, there were many other important players.

Dr. Carl A. Schenck was a German forester who succeeded Pinchot as manager of Vanderbilt's vast forest properties. For 14 years, Schenck worked to transform the land into what is today known as the 6,500-acre Pisgah National Forest. In 1898, he began the first forestry school in America, the Biltmore Forest School. Today one may visit this "cradle of forestry in America" in the Pisgah National Forest near the Asheville, North Carolina, area and see the actual buildings in which the first students of forestry learned their trade from Schenck. The first class graduated in 1913, and eventually the school was absorbed by Vanderbilt University in Nashville.

Carl Schenck, left.

Izaak Walton was a 17th-century English angler-conservationist who wrote the literary classic, *The Complete Angler.* The Izaak Walton League of America was founded to honor him in 1922 by 54 Chicago sportsmen who were alarmed by the deteriorating conditions of fishing streams due to uncontrolled industrial discharges, raw sewage and drained wetlands. The league is made up of hunters, anglers and other conservation-minded outdoor enthusiasts. I have to admit to being a proud member. Now with more than 50,000 members, the organization is influential in such areas as soil erosion, wetlands protection, clean air and the protection of several public lands, including the Upper Mississippi National Wildlife and Fish Refuge, the Everglades in Florida and the National Elk Refuge in Wyoming.

Charles S. Sargent is perhaps best known for his involvement with the Arnold Arboretum at Harvard University. During his 54 years with the arboretum, it grew from 120 acres to 265 acres and became a leading institution for research in botany, dendrology and horticulture. Sargent collected a group of landscape architects, photographers and writers who traveled the world chronicling plants and trees. As this group traveled, it wrote, keeping alive the public's imagination and interest in nature.

Frederick Law Olmsted (1822-1902) was a true believer in the beautification of cities and towns. The designer of Central Park in New York, Olmsted also was instrumental in designing parks in Boston, Chicago and Atlanta. Olmsted believed that the more visually pleasing a city was, the more people would want to live there and the happier they would be there. He wanted communities to be planned for the sole purpose of domestic life. He tried to link the city and country with rapid transit and designed suburbs with numerous "open air apartments" by which domestic activities could be moved outside the home. It could be argued that Olmsted was the inventor of what we call "urban forestry" today.

In 1845, Henry David Thoreau went to live and work at Walden Pond near Boston, where he stayed for two years,

Frederick Law Olmsted

FOREST HISTORY SOCIETY

keeping a journal of his thoughts and and his ideas about nature and society. These thoughts were published in a wonderful book, *Walden; or, Life in the Woods,* which remains an American literary classic. Thoreau was influenced by Ralph Waldo Emerson, whose essay in 1836, "Nature," proposed that everyone should seek a spiritually fulfilling relationship with the natural world. For his part, Thoreau condemned society's destruction of the forest, but he also noted with awe the forest's ability to renew itself.

Today Walden Pond is open to the public, acquired by the

Henry David Thoreau

commonwealth in 1922. However, by that time most of the wood had been cut down. Today most of the trees have grown back and a preservation effort, led by Don Henley of the Eagles, has been successful.

The first line of Joyce Kilmer's poem "Trees" is embedded in every schoolchild's head: "I think that I shall never see a poem lovely as a tree." Kilmer was killed in World War I. Legend has it that as he lay dying, he saw a tree on the crest of a hill a few hundred yards away, wrote the poem "Trees" and then breathed his last breath. It's a splendidly romantic story—except that "Trees" was published in 1914, and Kilmer was killed in 1918. In addition to his poem, Kilmer is memorialized in a 3,800-acre national park in North Carolina that contains one of the largest stands of old-growth trees in the eastern U.S.

By contrast, the "legend" of Johnny Appleseed is based in fact. Born John Chapman in 1774, Johnny Appleseed moved to Ohio in 1800 and started his apple-tree planting activities. No one really knows why, but for some reason he was compelled to roam an area of 100,000 miles in Pennsylvania, Ohio, Kentucky, Illinois and Indiana planting trees. He also sold apple seedlings for a "flip-penny bit," or about six-and-a-half cents. But money was not his motivation. He just did it.

In 1994 the last surviving apple tree planted by Johnny Appleseed was discovered in the town of Nova, Ohio. Representatives of the Famous & Historic Trees Project went there to supervise several hundred cuttings; now planted in a nursery outside Pelham, Tennessee, the new trees are thriving. That original tree, a Rambo apple tree, was almost felled in 1996 by a storm but is slowly showing signs of recovery.

Andreas Stihl, the "father of the chain saw," produced the world's first electric "tree-felling machine" in Germany in 1926. Three years later, he unveiled one of the first gasoline-powered chain saws. Following his invention, other manufacturers throughout the world latched onto the concept, spawning a multitude of companies selling chain saws. The impact of the chain saw on logging in America and the rest of the

Andreas Stihl

STIHL, INC.

world is obvious, and while most modern day harvesting is done with much bigger machinery, the chain saw is still in wide use today. Today, Stihl remains a leader in this arena and manufactures the world's top-selling brand of chain saws and cut-off machines, as well as a full line of garden equipment. Their products are sold by more than 30,000 dealers in more than 130 countries. The company also sponsors the annual "Stilh National Forestry Heroism Award," which recognizes an individual who has made an outstanding contribution or performed an extraordinary act in the realm of forestry that has positively affected mankind.

Franklin Delano Roosevelt also made a profound contribution to the forests. In an effort to relieve the economic hardships of the Depression, he created the Civilian Conservation Corps (CCC) that employed thousands of young men in a wide range of conservation, rehabilitation and construction projects in the national and state parks. In 1935, the National Park Service oversaw 600 CCC camps, 118 of them in national lands and 482 in state parks. When the economy recovered, the CCC's efforts continued. Regional offices, originally established to coordinate the CCC in the state parks, evolved in 1937 into a permanent regional structure for management of the National Park System. In addition, many of the landscape architects, foresters, biologists and archeologists stayed on with the Park Service. Roosevelt also established four new national parks: Great Smokey Mountains, Shenandoah, Isle Royale and Mammoth Cave.

There are so many more who have influenced people to stand up for our forests. The thing to remember is that you don't have to be a leader or spokesman for the forests. Your own actions are enough. Each of us reaps the benefits of trees; each of us should protect them.

Rachel Carson's book, *Silent Spring*, alerted Americans to the dark side of our industrial world and is credited with starting the environmental movement. We are now aware of the dangers of pesticides, but when the book was published in 1962, her words were viewed as heresy. *Silent Spring* reported

Aldo Leopold

on the types of poisons the chemical industry was pouring into our water systems, which Carson called "rivers of death." Her work also introduced the term "ecosystem" and was an impetus for the creation of the Environmental Protection Agency.

J. Sterling Morton is the father of Arbor Day, a holiday established in 1874 by the Nebraska legislature to encourage the prairie settlers to plant trees. The state's citizens responded by planting one million trees that year. Later, as the holiday was celebrated nationally, it was moved from April 10 to April 22 in honor of Morton's birthday. Arbor Day is now celebrated the last Friday in April.

Aldo Leopold received his instruction in forestry from Yale University in 1909 and spent 19 years working for the U.S. Forest Service. He is best known as the author of *A Sand County Almanac*. The book, published in 1949, is a volume of sketches and philosophical essays on the ecological attitude of man toward the land. Leopold developed the notion of a land ethic, asserting that it is wrong to disturb the balance of nature for any reason. He argued that it was man's duty to protect as much wildlife as possible in order to preserve the biological future of all species. The *Almanac*, published after his death, was amazingly influential as it put forth the notion that successful conservation meant taking the ethical sense of responsibility that humans assume among each other and extending it to nature.

CHAPTER SEVEN

☙

EARLY DAYS, OLD WAYS

"Paul Bunyan never replanted, or worried about erosion or ecosystems. He probably took early naturalists by the head and used them to grease his mighty skillet. On the other hand, without Paul Bunyan statues and memorabilia pulling the tourists to the forests, no one would ever see the magnificent trees that the modern tree farmer works so hard to protect."
~ Jeff Kirby, *Roadside America*

Paul Bunyan is one of America's great folk heroes. The legendary lumberjack possessed the strength, speed and skill that were needed to tame the forest and this land.

If there really was a Paul Bunyan, or even a man who inspired the great tales, it has yet to be proven, though the French-Canadians have claimed that Paul Bunyan actually lived in the western logging camps in the early 20th century. The legend of the mighty Bunyan and his giant blue ox, Babe, seems to have originated around the logging camps of Michigan, Wisconsin and Minnesota. Eventually, the tale grew so large that it was said he created Puget Sound, the Grand Canyon and the Black Hills with the swing of his ax.

The real loggers of this era were as worthy of mythical status as Paul Bunyan. The woodsmen, those who cut the trees, were known as "shanty boys," and they were all heroes. The work was backbreakingly tough and required a lot of fortitude.

Lumberjacks worked six days a week, cutting, hauling and piling logs. For this labor, in the mid-1800s, they generally received from $20 to $26 a month. In Santa Cruz, California, in the late 1800s, the loggers received $1.50 a day, but 50 cents went back to the lumber company for room and board.

They lived in primitive logging camps where, since most of the logging took place in the winter, conditions were particularly harsh. The cabins were cold, drafty and far away from civilization. Visits to towns were rare, probably weeks apart.

The main camp was usually built around a fire pit, which supplied warmth and a cooking fire, and was made of large notched logs, such as spruce, chinked with moss and mud,

Early logging camp.

usually making a 20-by-20-foot square. Everything was usually put together without nails since the camp wasn't supposed to be permanent. The roof was made of cedar shakes held down by long poles across each tier and tied down with cedar and spruce roots and bark strips. Usually there was a square hole in the center of the roof for the smoke to go out. There was generally one window and a door.

It wasn't unusual for all the men to sleep in one community bed. A deacon seat, a half log smoothed on one side, served as both a footboard and a seat. The mattress was often made of pine needles. Not until 1917, when the loggers went on strike, did they get real mattresses. They usually slept in their long underwear and a boot sometimes served as a pillow. Ticks, lice and other bugs were constant companions.

The kitchen sink was a hollowed log. They ate four meals a day, including pancakes, pickled beets, oiled codfish, beans, biscuits and tea. Clothes were dried over a fire on a long "stink" pole held up by two forked stakes. Loggers, it was often said, could be smelled half a mile away.

Besides the shanty men, there were cooks, blacksmiths and other support personnel living at the camps. Many of the lumberjacks were immigrants, who often had traveled as a group from the same hometown in Europe, seeking work. Although Canadians comprised a large part of this international element, men from Scandinavia soon had a significant presence in the camps as well.

In 1882, a young boy wrote a letter to his father, a preacher in Madison, Wisconsin, about his one season in the logging camps. The letter, now called "He Didn't Like it," was first published in the *Chippewa Herald*.

We have to get up at about 2:30, get breakfast at three, and then walk four miles to work and take a cold dinner with us, and get back to the shanty, all the way from seven to nine o'clock. So you see we have pretty long days in the woods....

After supper we roll into our soft, downy couch of lousy blankets and lay and listen to ... snoring in seven different languages, mostly imported—professional snorers from Germany and Norway .... while the beautiful odor of wet socks and foot rags is heard in the near distance, and finally fall sleep to slow music, only to be awakened in a few minutes by the melodious voice of the cook singing, 'roll out your dead bodies, daylight in the swamp ....'"

There was little to amuse the men. Believe it or not, some of the logging camps, like those in Santa Cruz, banned liquor. So the men found their own ways to pass what limited free time they had. They gambled, told stories, sang and enjoyed contests of skill and strength, turning many of the skills needed in their jobs into competitive games. They had ax-throwing contests and logrolling challenges, where two men would walk on the log as it rotated and try to avoid falling into the water.

Today, there are several places—historic museums honoring the lumberjacks and colleges with forestry programs, mainly— that still showcase the skills of the lumberjacks. Stihl, the well-known German and U.S. retail maker of chain saws and other power tools, carries on those traditions with a televised show called "Timbersports."

We're not sure they actually did this back in the 1800s, but one contest that takes place today is springboard chopping, where a person climbs a nine-foot pole and while balancing on a narrow springboard, chops off the top of the pole. In another game, "the quarter split," a competitor is given a small piece of wood with a dot in the middle. The object is to split the wood into four pieces, each of which has some part of the dot on it. The most efficient way to split wood is in four exact

FOREST HISTORY SOCIETY

Tools of the trade.

TEMPLE-INLAND CORP.

quarters so the skill could have come in handy for these early lumberjacks.

Until machinery came into use in the late 1880s, the vast majority of the trees were cut in the winter because the frozen ground made it easier to move them to their destination, the river. One man wielding a simple ax would chop away until the tree fell. In the late 1800s came the crosscut saw, with a handle on each end, used by two men who sawed back and forth in rhythm, slowly slicing through virgin timber, almost like they were rowing a boat.

The loggers would cut the trees in a path toward the river. They would clear the path and build a skid road, which consisted of small lengths of logs laid side by side on a graded roadbed.

Once a tree was felled, the shanty boy used a cant hook – a pole with a hook attached to the end, also known as a cant dog – to lift, turn and pry logs, maneuvering them into position. Also used was a single dingle, which was a swivel hook on a pole. Axes were used to cut off limbs and branches.

The shanty boys would drag the logs over the frozen ground and icy roads with log chains—often with swamp hooks attached—directly to nearby river banks. Another alternative was to place the logs on large sleds. At first, oxen, working in teams of four, six or eight, pulled the sleds laden with logs; later, sled teams of horses did the job.

The men also helped nature along. Poles were placed crossways on the skid trail, and the lead end of the log tapered slightly with an ax. Lard, or whatever greasy fluid was available, would then be applied to the skids to make them slicker and help the logs slide better. Thus we have the term "greasing the skids." It also gave us the term "skid row," which now connotes a place for people down on their luck. But the term was first used for a street in Seattle where the logs were sent down to a sawmill.

After felling, timber had to be moved.

Dangerous work.

At the riverbanks the tree was cut and further stripped of any branches. Then the logs were piled up on backgrounds and stockpiled until spring. The lumber company that owned the logs would brand the logs with its logo using a marking hammer.

When spring came, the melting snow and rains signaled the beginning of the dangerous log drives. At this time the log drivers, also known as river hogs, would break the ties holding the logs (called rollways), which released the logs into the river. The deafening sound must have shaken the earth.

Using pike poles (a steel point attached to a very long handle) and riding in a special boat—and sometimes balancing on the logs themselves—the drivers had to keep those logs moving down the ice-packed rivers. Logjams were frequent and could extend for several miles upstream. The drivers had to

Big wheels in operation.

figure out how to manipulate the logs around in a way that would get them moving again. River drivers were forced to jump into the freezing and fast-flowing rivers using their tools and skills to keep the logs rolling. Sometimes dynamite was used to this end. All too often, the drivers drowned or were crushed when the logs started moving again.

Thousands of logs would pass downstream during these drives, so many that the Penobscot River in Maine at one time was called the "river of logs." But as the forests of New York and Maine had become depleted, Michigan raced to fill the gap. By the 1860s, Michigan had become the country's biggest producer of lumber. As demand escalated, the challenge was finding a way to cut trees and market them all year long.

In the 1870s, technology helped solve the problem. A

Michigan native, Silas Overpack, led the way by inventing the Big Wheels, which was a set of enormous wheels drawn by a team of horses. Logs were chained underneath the axle. Not only was it easy to keep the wheels moving, but the Big Wheels, unlike the sleds, didn't require snow or frozen ground to operate. That meant that logging was now a year-round enterprise.

Big Wheels came in three sizes and could carry logs from 12 to 100 feet in length – enough to total 1,000 to 2,000 board feet of lumber in a single load. The machine's wheels were always painted a bright red. Big Wheels were also known as logging wheels, Michigan wheels and bummer carts and were used until about the 1920s.

Another invention that helped turn logging into a year-round business was the narrow-gauge railroad. Trains could be used in place of sleds for the short runs to the riverside banking grounds, or the river drive itself, by transporting the logs to a mainline railroad depot. The trains allowed the lumberjacks to go deeper into the woods, something they couldn't do previously, as demand for timber dictated.

The small steam donkey was another machine that got the wood to the rivers 12 months a year. The donkey consisted of a steam boiler and steam engine connected to a winch and mounted on a "donkey" sled. The donkeys were dragged with a winch line—a rope attached to a hand-powered or engine-driven hoisting machine that had a drum around it so the rope could be wound around it as a load was lifted.

In rapid fashion, the donkeys were used both for yarding (moving the logs from where the tree was cut to an assembly point) and also skidding or dragging the logs down the skid trail to the river. An 11-man donkey crew could skid five carloads of logs or 80,000 board feet of timber a day.

Another important invention was the Lombard steam log hauler, devised by Alvin Lombard in 1914. His invention was

Mules and oxen did hard labor in the early days.

Steam donkey, c. 1894

the predecessor of machines like tanks, bulldozers and tractors that roll on a belt rather than just wheels. The first log haulers were steered by horses; eventually, a steersman sat on the front of the sled, guiding the hauler by a large iron wheel that turned the runners. Believe it or not, the haulers had no brakes, despite the fact that they could carry 300 tons at a time. The logs were carried on sleds connected like a train, usually four to ten sleds joined together at one time going four to five miles an hour. Downhill it could go as fast as 20 miles an hour—and don't forget, no brakes!

By whatever means, the logs ultimately arrived at sawmills where they were sawed, sliced and shipped.

At the sawmill, lumber was first "pit-sawed" by two men

Technology arrives in the sawmills.

FOREST HISTORY SOCIETY

with a long saw that had crosshandles at each end. A log was placed over the pit. One sawyer stood on top of it to pull the saw up while the other man, the pit man, stood in the pit to pull the saw down. They would usually saw 12 to 14 boards a day. Eventually pit saws were connected to a drive shaft and powered by water instead of hand. The saw moved up and down very slowly, cutting only on the down stroke. Later gang saws, which are fitted with several blades for making simultaneous parallel cuts, were used. A gang saw is similar to the machine that slices bread.

Just around the time of the Civil War, the lumber industry started to see the first signs of serious technology. Water-powered mills were still common then, but steam saws—either up-and-down or circular—were just coming into use. Steam saws were so efficient that it became necessary to come up with faster ways to handle both the logs and the sawed lumber in order to prevent pile-ups and delays. Within a decade, just about every sawmill had started changing over to the new ways.

The first circular saws had wide blades that yielded mountains of sawdust. Not very strong, these saws vibrated as they went through the log. The cutting was so uneven that they "more nearly resembled washboards than lumber," according to a story by Marian Quinlan in an essay called "Lumbering in Michigan." Soon the kinks were worked out, and the widespread adoption of the band saw in the 1880s further reduced waste. Now logs were cut with a saw made with a thin band of steel—a continuous belt that cut both rapidly and efficiently. These saws could cut as much as 10,000 feet a day. In the 1800s, the sawed lumber sold for $20 per 1000 board foot.

From the sawmills, the green, rough lumber went directly to the rafting sheds where men piled them into cribs. These cribs – usually 28 of them – were then fastened together into rafts. Using eight long oars for steering, the raftsmen guided

Early band saw in operation.

TEMPLE-INLAND CORP.

the unwieldy craft down the nearest waterways. The men cooked and slept on the raft, even pitching small tents. Eventually the rafts would meet up with a large river raft that was waiting on a major river, for further distribution either by river or train.

Given that even the most sophisticated tools were primitive by today's standards, the amount to wood these men cut down and processed is mind-boggling. For instance, by 1832, Bangor, Maine, had become the largest shipping port for lumber in the world. At times, as many as 3,000 ships were anchored waiting for their lumber. Between 1832 and 1888, more than 8.7 billion board feet of lumber was shipped from that port.

Like textile towns before them, communities grew up around the mills. It was not unusual for the lumber company to control everything—the houses, shops and jobs. Mill hands worked long hours in bad conditions. The mills were smelly and dirty, with sawdust creating a permanent cloud in the air. Workers often lost fingers and eyesight in these hazardous conditions. Fires were an ever-present danger. Although mill workers were paid more than loggers—about $30 to $50 a month—they sometimes had to provide their own room and board. More often than not, they also had families to support.

In these towns, lumbering was the only real business, with all else supporting it. Everyone's livelihoods, from the shop-keepers to the blacksmith to the schoolmarm, depended on the success of the loggers and a strong market for the lumber.

It was a recipe for disaster.

Unfortunately, in the early years, poor harvesting methods were used. When the land had been cleared of trees, the timber companies had no further interest in it. They just packed up and moved elsewhere where the forests were still untapped.

The stories of timber mill towns dying out parallel the early devastation of our forests. The sad tale traveled from Maine all the way across the country until it hit the Pacific Northwest and British Columbia

The old tales of mighty deeds, sacrifice and adventure around the early years of logging are a proud part of this country's history. In today's world, with all the machines, we don't need a giant's strength. But the men and women who go out into the forests and harvest the trees and work the saw mills are just as hardworking and admirable as ol' Paul Bunyan. And fortunately, the dreary legacy of deserted mill towns, horrendous working conditions and ruined forests is no longer being perpetuated by today's timber industry.

CHAPTER EIGHT

⌒

MODERN DAYS, NEW WAYS

"The best friend on Earth of man is the tree:
When we use the tree respectfully and economically,
we have one of the greatest resources of the earth."
~ Frank Lloyd Wright

The pioneering loggers who cut the trees to make way for our country's development surely wouldn't recognize their modern counterparts.

Today's logging technicians sit in air-conditioned cabins directing machines to cut and delimb the trees and get them to the lumber mill. Forest harvesting is a series of automated steps that turn a tree into lumber, paper or wood byproducts. In contrast to the horrible waste of past years, today's forest companies use every inch of the tree and take care to disturb the environment as little as possible. Though it is still a hard and dangerous job, for the most part today's forest workers earn good salaries and benefits and the work conditions are closely monitored.

Logging nowadays is more than just cutting trees and hauling them to the mill. Professional loggers must take into account safety, productivity, environmental and legal considerations, forest management practices and profitability. A lot of work is done even before one tree is cut. Today, most responsible forest companies and tree farmers alike hire licensed foresters—modern-day Gifford Pinchots—to walk the land, look over the trees and become familiar with the wildlife, taking many factors into consideration before making decisions about harvesting. No matter who owns the land or how big the property is, it is essential to have a plan.

First, the entire area must be inspected to make sure that the land—often called a "stand"—is not home to an endangered species. Depending on the part of the country, the presence of such species as the Canada lynx, the flatwoods salamander, the bald eagle, the Karner blue butterfly, spotted owl or the red cockaded woodpecker must be taken into account. Also, other factors such as wetlands, creek or river bottoms and other sensitive areas must be considered. Often a company's hands are tied concerning tree cutting because of the ecological impact. Sometimes trees can still be harvested, but extreme care must be taken over which trees are cut and how the land is disturbed.

Not only do foresters protect any endangered wildlife, they ensure that the cutting won't harm the environment in other ways. Standards within the forestry community ensure a responsible harvest. Best management practices, or BMPs, are a set of guidelines that address this issue. Following the contour of the land to prevent erosion, scattering limbs properly, and generally making as little an impact as possible on the land during harvest, are all planned out ahead of time.

Responsible landowners also make sure that a buffer zone of trees, called a streamside management zone (SMZ), remains in order to prevent erosion, maintain water quality, and keep needed shade and nutrients by the stream, creek or river for fish and animals. In addition, these SMZs provide a visually pleasing forest.

Many companies and private landowners also insist on aesthetic management zones, which means a forested area is left alongside highways or other appropriate locations. These zones make our highways much more attractive than they would be if the trees were cut right up to the roads.

CLEAR-CUTTING

While many methods exist to remove trees from any given stand, there are two main ways of harvesting trees—clear-cutting and selective cutting. Clear-cutting removes all the trees from a stand. Now, there are some who shudder at the very thought of a stand of trees suddenly becoming barren. We've all seen pictures of land looking like an electric razor went through and gave it a buzz cut, with little stubs sticking out of the ground and animals forlornly looking for a home.

But honestly, folks, the reality is that in some cases it is by far the best thing to do for the health and productivity of the forest and sometimes, at least for a period of time, is best for other considerations such as wildlife. So much depends on the particular situation, and of course replanting after a clear-cut within a reasonable time is essential. Another important factor is the way a clear-cut is conducted, and the size of the tract in question. Certainly clear-cutting is not always called for, nor do I advocate it over selective cutting, which I personally prefer in most cases. But there are certain instances where clear-cutting and starting over is without a doubt the best thing to do, as in the following example from my own experience.

Several years ago I purchased a 330-acre tract of land that was adjacent to our property. I intended to leave the property intact, restore a beautiful old home and add the tract to our existing land. It was a struggle for me to swing the deal, because at that time there were no Rolling Stones or Eric

Clapton tours coming up, and I had to borrow a significant amount of money from the bank. Many of the improvements on our land, like the horse barn and the lake, came in part from the proceeds of tours I've done. (Some of my friends, for instance, jokingly call the lake we built the Unplugged Lake, thanks to my playing with Eric on the *Unplugged* album, TV show and tour.)

Anyway, one of the stands on the tract—about 30 acres or so—was a stagnant stand of loblolly pine planted about 25 years before I bought the land. These were rather poor quality trees in a stand facing a public road. The tract could have been easily developed for residential property with a good thinning, creating an opportunity to sell smaller tracts and make a tidy profit in the process. But this would not have been the best decision for the quality of the stand in terms of good forestry management, which was my goal, and I had no interest in selling it for development. My long-range plan was to grow quality timber and have plenty of edge for the wildlife. So the best thing for me to do was to harvest all of it and replant better quality trees, and then manage them properly.

It's not unlike hair that's been damaged by too much coloring and blow-drying. Sometimes it's better to chop it all off and start over, then grow your hair out the way you want it— healthy and beautiful. Same thing, actually.

The point is again, that clear-cutting doesn't need to be a dirty word, and in my opinion, folks need to be a lot more open-minded about it. There are many justifications for clear-cutting. Clearly, it is the most efficient way to harvest trees. Cutting a stand that has been grown specifically for harvest is no different than harvesting acres of corn, soybeans or other crops. When the crop is ready for market, it is picked or cut and shipped, and then the resource is renewed.

Temple-Inland Forests, based in Diboll, Texas, provides a

good example of how clear-cutting can be done properly. Temple-Inland manages about 2.2 million acres of forestlands in Texas, Louisiana, Alabama and Georgia. About 6 percent of that land is harvested annually, with about 3 percent being clear-cut. The average size of a stand that is clear-cut is 43 acres. All the tracts of Temple-Inland clear-cut land are reforested within two years, creating new stands of future forests. Just think about that—within two years, that stand of land has living trees on it, and after a few years, when the stand has grown a bit, one would be hard pressed to even see it had been clear-cut.

In fact, for several years after a clear-cut, there is a whole new group of wildlife thriving. Since the land now gets full sunlight, new varieties of plants, herbs and animals are attracted to the sun-kissed land. With these shrubs comes a different type of animal that can't exist in the shaded area of a forest. A growing clear-cut stand would provide a great home for bear, deer, grouse, young turkey, quail, elk, moose and many other species, depending on the area. Of course, as the trees grow back, the habitat may be less friendly to those animals, as the crowns of the newly planted trees begin to close and shade out the forest floor. But even then the area can be useful as travel lanes and shelter for various animals and birds. As the trees mature, they provide a welcome home for species such as squirrel, possum, adult turkeys and raccoons, as well as providing safe travel underneath the canopy.

It's important to make a distinction between clear-cutting and deforestation. Deforestation occurs when trees are cut and there is no intent to replace them. It must be said that such tactics were employed in years past when loggers didn't know any better. Today we do know better, and there is no excuse for deforestation when it comes to managing forests. But let's give some examples of modern-day deforestation.

Think of a new shopping mall being developed. Though I'm certainly not opposed to smart growth for our country, any new development like a shopping mall, high-rise building, strip mall, etc., is true deforestation. So is road building, and the building of a sports stadium, or any type of building activity that takes away trees without putting them back. Even the transition from forest to agriculture is deforestation. Now in some cases the landscaping can and does include the replanting of some trees for aesthetic purposes, and then we get into Urban Forestry, which is another chapter. But it is important to note that these days most companies and individuals that are in the business of growing trees for the use of man are managing their forests wisely, and when harvests occur, replanting is right behind that harvest.

Properly done, there can be tree harvesting and reforestation with clear-cutting. In many instances, such as the example of my own land, it can actually improve the future stand quality, growth, genetics and species composition.

Many would argue that clear-cutting erodes the soil, but that isn't true. Erosion has almost nothing to do with how much wood is removed, but everything to do with the method and care of the removal of the trees. When a tree is cut, the roots remain deep in the soil, keeping it intact. Erosion can and does sometimes occur—from improper skidding trails, bad logging roads and failure to follow the contour of the land. However, if a logger does his job correctly, staying well away from streamside areas, skidding the felled trees with care and building access roads sparingly and carefully, following BMPs and protecting SMZs as mentioned earlier, then no negative impact on the soil will occur from the operation.

In my opinion, the most dangerous thing we face in managing our forests is urban sprawl. I would ask the question: "Where is the biodiversity in that concrete and asphalt?"

There is so much that we can do in our inner cities where abandoned buildings and lots exist that need to be developed and occupied, and if we concentrate on fixing up these places, perhaps we won't need to take away so much agricultural and forest land for the developments that are ever-encroaching our countryside.

SELECTIVE CUTTING

Another method of harvesting timber on a longer-term basis is selective lumbering. Before the machines start grinding, the logger, the landowner, a forester and the forest company (if the landowner is selling the trees to a forest company) should meet to discuss objectives. Every detail of the logging operation ought to be covered and agreed upon before a tree is touched. Called a harvest "prescription," the loggers are given precise instructions on what to cut —how many trees and what kind—and what to leave alone. In most cases, the trees that are to be removed are marked with paint . . . one mark about chest high and one at the base of the tree below the sawing level so that after the harvest there is a "record" of the trees taken out. The opposite method is called "leave-tree marking," in which the trees to be left are given the paint. This method is useful when the stand is so dense that it would take an inordinate amount of time and effort to mark all the trees to take. Each successive cut should improve the age distribution, density and quality of the stand. In most well-thought-out selective harvests, the lowest quality trees are removed and "mature" trees are cut only when they decline in health.

Timber companies usually want trees of the same age and size, and this is called even-aged forest management. For the Southern pine, depending on soil types, tree quality and other factors, the ideal age for a first thinning could be anywhere from about 12 to 18 years. Depending on the goal for the stand, hardwoods may be removed to allow for more sunlight. In other instances, certain hardwoods may be left in the stand for the benefit of wildlife or simply for forest diversity.

An important part of the prescription is the basal area. The basal area per acre is a way to measure tree density within a given stand and is expressed in square feet per acre. For example, a 30-square-foot basal area means that if you cut down the trees on an acre at a height of 4.5 feet (known as diameter breast height, or dbh for short) and added the surface area of all the stump tops, there would be 30 square feet worth of trees. It can also say how far apart the trees should be from each other.

A method for a first thinning of pines in the Southeast that is popular these days is "every fifth row and some in-between." While initial spacing of trees can vary from about 6' x 9' (i.e., trees six feet apart in rows nine feet apart) to 10' x 10' (435-800 trees per acre), depending on soil quality and other factors, a good average spacing is 6' x 10', resulting in 726 trees per acre. Given this spacing, upon the maturity of the pines to the point of a first thinning, taking all the trees in every fifth row gives the logger some room to maneuver. Then some of the lesser trees within the other rows may be removed, leaving the best to grow for a healthy forest. One of the advantages of selective logging is that almost every tree is treated individually. If done properly, no tree is unnecessarily taken down. Trees that are diseased, crooked, suppressed, forked or otherwise damaged are removed, and the best are left to grow, therefore upgrading the quality of the forest as time goes on.

TIMBER!

Once the prescription is agreed upon and written up, and all the other necessary steps taken, then the logging crews can

Forwarder in operation.

TEMPLE-INLAND CORP.

prepare for the harvest. Safety, efficiency and doing as little harm as possible to the environment are all priorities with the crew. If no road exists to the site, the first order of business is to put a road in so that machines and equipment can enter. Also, areas for delimbing and loading are created, which are generally called loading decks.

In most conventional logging operations in America, trees are cut by a machine called a feller-buncher. The feller-buncher is a large three- or four-wheel or track-mounted machine with a cabin for the operator, hydraulic arms and a vertical pole with "claws" for holding the tree when cutting. At the bottom of the pole is a holding platform with a large saw or chain protruding below it. The feller-buncher operator drives up to the tree, pushes a few buttons, moves the stick-shift control, and, like a giant robot gathering stalks of asparagus, the claws grab the tree. Another control activates the saw and before you can yell "Timber!" the saw rips through the bottom of the tree, virtually at ground level. The feller-buncher holds the trunk on a platform above the saw and goes to the next tree. Depending on the width of the tree, the harvester can hold a number of tree trunks—just like bunches of asparagus!

The machine then takes the trunks to a central area in the woods where the delimber takes over. There are several different kinds of delimbers used in conventional logging operations today.

Two versions of what is known as a "stroke" delimber utilize cranes to pick up a tree from a stack. One type, called a pull-through, loader-operated delimber, pushes the tree through a chamber where grinders remove the branches. The second type, known as a self-contained stroke delimber, features a sliding mechanism that travels back and forth to achieve the same results. Both can turn trees into transportable poles in seconds.

Another method is to use a "gate delimber," which is a large, heavy "grid" of iron piping that a group of trees are backed into, knocking off the limbs. This can cause a large pit where the operation takes place and also creates a large pile of limbs that must be dealt with in some way.

Regardless of the method, the delimbed trunks are piled high in a stack waiting for a loader with a high mechanical arm and grapple to pick them up and put them on the trucks to be taken to the mill.

Today, enlightened loggers do not leave the site without trying to minimize the damage. Rather than leave piles of leaves and limbs in a stack, those logging companies that practice good harvesting methods will scatter the debris back over the roads, thus reducing land damage and erosion while encouraging plant growth.

Forwarding System

A system that is quite often used in Europe, but to a much lesser degree here in the U.S. is the forwarding system. In this method, the feller machine not only cuts the tree down initially, but delimbs it right afterwards, then further cuts it into pre-determined lengths and stacks the logs in the woods. Then the forwarder machine comes behind the feller, loads the logs up, and takes them to the mill. I personally like this method very much, as during the operation the limbs are scattered immediately throughout the forest floor, acting as a protective covering for the machines to "walk" over, thus lessening the impact on the soil. Also, this "walking" helps to crunch the litter underneath the tracks of the machine, making decomposition occur sooner and "composting" the forest floor. The newest of these machines carry satellite and computer technology. I witnessed a harvest in Sweden in 1995 on an off day during the "Voodoo Lounge" tour with the Stones that used this technology. The feller machine received direct satellite signals from the mill to determine the length of the logs being cut. If the mill had enough inventory of a certain length of logs, then a signal was sent to the machine telling it to cut another length. The operator of the feller would also be alerted to this change, but unless there was a problem of some sort, he wouldn't need to do anything himself other than make sure the machine was doing what it was being "told" to do. I found this fascinating, and this method by far is the "friendliest" to the forest, having the lowest impact on the forest floor. I wish this method was used more in the U.S., but it is slow in coming – for a couple of reasons. First, the equipment is very expensive, and it takes quite a big financial commitment from a logging company to change to this method. Also, it's a bit slower than the current conventional method of skidding and loading decks, thereby reducing profits. In my opinion, we should try to create incentives for this kind of harvesting and thinning operation because of the low impact on the environment.

OLD-FASHIONED WAYS STILL WORK!

Although I've described the primary ways that trees are cut, there are still others in use. While very rare, some operations still use chain saws and mules to help harvest trees; at the other end of the spectrum, others use helicopters for the same purpose.

Small companies and independent landowners may use adapted farm tractors or mules for several reasons. First, it's cheaper using this kind of equipment to cut and drag the logs than it is to pay hundreds of thousands of dollars for more sophisticated machines. Some landowners may like the romance of going out into the forest and cutting the trees in a really hands-on way, and many who use these methods also still cut trees with power saws. This method, called open-felling, is very much like the way it was done in the good old days. Using the feller-buncher, the trees don't fall, but are rather laid down. With the open method, they fall.

I've used this method here at Charlane to cut down trees that have been struck by lightning, or have died due to insects, or perhaps have been blown down by wind. Whatever the reason, rather than let these trees go to waste, we cut them down, then further cut them into lengths depending on the need or depending on what the tree might make. Then, using a home-made grapple that we built for my John Deere tractor, we bring the logs up to a central "deck," where we use a Woodmiser brand portable sawmill to saw them into lumber. We've salvaged enough of these otherwise lost trees to build a 40-foot by 78-foot horse barn, along with a shop and storage facility, to build over a mile of wooden fencing for our horses, and to

Chuck dragging timber to his Woodmiser sawmill . . .

. . . and this barn is the result.

renovate the interior of one of our lodges. We have plans to do even more. Not only have we saved money on the cost of the lumber we've used, but I must say that it's a special feeling to know that these projects were done using our own resources, especially since these trees would have otherwise been left to rot in the woods.

If the open-cutting, tractor or mule methods seem retro, the helicopter method is definitely the 21st-century type. The first use of a helicopter to carry logs occurred in Scotland in 1956; in the U.S. it was in 1971, in the Plumas National Forest in California. Around this same time, forest companies in British Columbia took to using helicopters. It wasn't until the 1990s, though, that the practice became common.

There are several advantages to using helicopters. The first is environmental. Since there is no new road clearing on a mountain face, less land is disturbed. There is also less watershed

A modern-day heli-logging operation.

damage. The cutting is selective, and can target particular trees, like cedars, that bring in an above-average market price.

Heli-logging usually occurs in the Pacific Northwest and Canada in areas that previously were unrealistic and inaccessible for logging. The loggers and machines could get up the mountain slopes, but they couldn't figure out how to get the huge trees down the slopes safety.

Now loggers, often using existing roads, cut the trees and mill them into commercial-size logs on site. Once enough timber has been cut, helicopters carefully fly above, hook up chains to the logs and carry the wood off. It's no easy task. One 41-foot Douglas fir log, 48 inches in diameter, can weigh 24,000 pounds!

Other advantages are efficiency and effectiveness. The volume of wood extracted is substantially greater per shift than with a conventional operation. In addition, crews can be relocated quickly. Heli-logging operations can function even in winter when most other logging practices shut down, and the method is also useful in swamp areas where ground maneuvering can be difficult. A couple of downsides of heli-logging: the expense and the element of danger. As you might imagine, it can be very expensive to hire the chopper and crew, and this method is mostly used in very special situations. Accidents have happened in the past, but this technology has come a long way and certainly has its place in modern logging.

TODAY'S SAWMILLS

Regardless of how the logs are cut and transported, eventually they end up at a sawmill or a paper mill. Some wood species, such as high-grade oak, cedar and black walnut, are highly prized for interior uses, gunstocks, artistic carvings, veneers and fine furniture. Other species might be used for lumber products such as studs, framing and the like.

Today's sawmills are wonders of automation, modern science and efficiency. When the logs first arrive at the sawmill, they are stored in water or in a place with a sprinkler system over them to prevent fungus and rotting. Again, the grandfathers of today's mill workers would hardly recognize the operation. Where dozens of men were once necessary for the cutting and moving of the logs, today just a handful are needed.

The logs are lifted from the storage areas by cranes, called log-side lifters, where they are quickly loaded onto an electronic steel-sided conveyor belt. The logs are further delimbed and then enter the first of at least two computer-scanning devices, including laser measurement, so that ultimately an operator high above in a control tower can determine what is the best, most efficient use of that log.

The operator, looking a bit like Captain Kirk at his desk, sits in a small air-conditioned cabin with a huge chair facing several television monitors that show the action taking place down below. In addition, there are several panels with various colored buttons, all with a very precise purpose. Computers do millions of calculations in the blink of an eye to determine the best way to saw the log. The operator, who is watching and absorbing the split-second action, makes equally split-second decisions regarding the wood.

Any trees with deficiencies, such as those not straight enough, are instantly eliminated. Some mills have special computers to decide what is best for a crooked log, but some depend on the operator to make the final decision on that log's fate. If a crooked log can't be salvaged, the operator, with a flick of a switch, opens up the conveyor belt and it falls straight into a bin that goes directly to the chipping process.

Along the way, metal detectors scan the logs for any metal

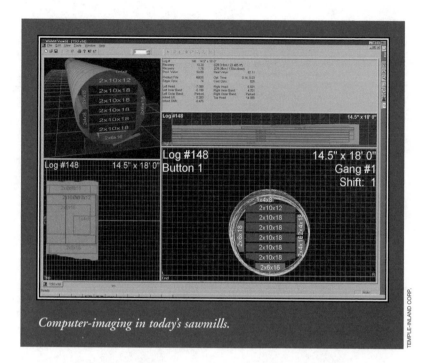

Computer-imaging in today's sawmills.

– like nails – that might wreak havoc on the blades of the saws. This is also figured into the decision regarding the optimal use of the log.

After the first go-round with the computer, the log is then put back on the conveyer belt for a second computer reading, with the log fully rotated, for the final determination as to how the log will be cut. There are an amazing number of variations—a sort of statistical nightmare—all made within a matter of seconds. Based on the computer's assessment, the log is then carried to the cutting process where, again in a matter of seconds, it is cut precisely the way the computer ordered. One log could make several 8-by-10 planks as well as 5-by-7s, 2-by-3s, or whatever combination would be the most efficient. Each log does not have to yield the same output.

Multiple monitors track the sawmilling operation.

The wood is dried using a computer-controlled kiln to achieve the correct moisture content. Following the drying and conditioning process, the wood is then graded, sorted, stacked and readied for shipping.

The mill at Temple-Inland's Diboll sawmill, which, as of this writing, is a true state-of-the-art mill, handles between 9,000 to 9,500 bucked logs per day (i.e., logs that have been cut for optimal use but that have not yet gone through the scanner process). Tips or butts of the log may, for instance, be cut off to produce a straight and even log. About nine bucked logs per minute are processed. The mill produces 62,000 to 65,000 pieces of lumber a day, which comes out to 675,000 to 725,000 board feet. Most logs are between seven to 12 inches in diameter. If Temple-Inland were to build that sawmill today, the cost could easily top $50 million.

While the main buck of the tree is used for making lumber, the rest is used for other purposes. Nothing is wasted. All discarded wood cut from the trees, as well as rejected logs, is quickly turned into wood chips and blown from the sawmill to another mill, such as one that makes fiber products.

FIBERBOARDS

Fiberboard, used for the outsides and roofs of houses, is also a lumber substitute for trim applications and an innovative and amazing way to use wasted wood leftovers. The raw material comes from the sawmill and is sent to digesters, where the chips are steam "cooked" with up to 200 pounds of pressure to soften the chips and free the wood's sugars. When they enter the steam cookers, the chips are 2 percent fiber and 98 percent wood. The first duty is to "de-water" the material, which is done by free drainage, then by vacuum and pressure from a press.

The cooked chips are fed into refiners where they are ground into fine fiber. The fiber is washed to remove wood sugars, which become the consistency of molasses and are sold to cattle and horse feed makers as a livestock feed ingredient.

The fiber sheet of "chips" is then cut to a predetermined size by high-pressure water jets. Each section of formed fiber is referred to as a mat. Mat sizes usually are 12 feet wide and 16 to 27 feet long. At this point, the mats are now half-water, half-fiber. They are fed into multi-level gas-fired dryers or kilns where they will take up to three hours to dry. Also during this process they are stamped or molded with a simulated wood grain. After the final drying is done, the fiberboard is given some strength-enhancing and waterproofing chemicals. Now it's time for storage and shipping.

CYCLE OF A TREE'S LIFE

Thus we have the cycle of today's logging operation. And it must come full circle. The trees must be cut, processed and used. But more trees must be planted. The last part is vital to the health of the forest and our future. Sustainability is a big issue and one that we will get to in an upcoming chapter. But it is important to know that reforestation is a vital part of any logging operation.

Weyerhaeuser, which manages 7.5 million acres of private working forests in the U.S., and another 33.8 million of publicly owned forestland in Canada, plants 33 million seedlings a year in the southern U.S. alone! It grows 270 million seedlings annually in nurseries and greenhouses.

Temple-Inland plants 22 million pine seedlings on 30,000 acres of company land each winter in Texas and Louisiana alone. In Georgia and Alabama, an average of 14 million seedlings is planted on about 18,000 acres annually. The company also grows 55,000 bald cypress trees annually for the National Tree Trust that distributes these trees free of charge to communities and organizations across the country.

Plum Creek Timber Company, a publicly-traded *Real Estate Investment Trust*, manages 8.1 million acres of forestland, a little over half of which is in the South. Each year, the company plants 125 million seedlings and allows many more millions of trees to regenerate naturally. For instance, on each forested acre, the company leaves 10 to 15 trees (called a "seed tree cut") to provide new trees the old-fashioned, Mother Nature-way of creating for the next generation. Weyerhaeuser, Temple-Inland and Plum Creek Timber are not alone. Most timber companies and private landowners that manage and harvest their forestland are quick to site prep and replant those lands. Most timber companies have their lands and wood procurement systems certified by independent auditors to ensure that they are adhering to sustainable forestry practices.

After all, the only way to have trees for the future is to plant trees today.

CHAPTER NINE

⌒

URBAN FORESTS

"Acts of creation are ordinarily reserved for Gods and poets. To plant a pine, one need only own a shovel."
~ Aldo Leopold

Through much of this book we've talked about forests — large tracts of trees of various or singular species. We certainly, however, can't forget about the trees where most people live — in the cities, towns and suburban areas. Urban forests face just as many challenges as our state and national parks. In fact, maybe more, because as increasing numbers move to the cities and suburbs, more trees are removed to make way for the settlers — a situation not much different from the 1800s.

The number of trees being destroyed in some places is astonishing. In Atlanta, which is often called the City of Trees, an average of about 50 acres of trees a day for the past 25 years have been lost to development. And it's happening all over the country and world. Trees in some of our cities are being cut down in massive numbers, are being disregarded in development plans, or simply die from neglect. This is a complicated problem, and there are no easy answers.

For example, consider temperature. Urban areas are usually

warmer – a condition known as the "urban heat island" effect. The heat from the buildings, cars and people is trapped, unable to leave, and intensified, just like in roasting meat. Is this a problem trees can help solve, or are trees victimized by urban heat? We know that trees cool the air around them, and I've read a lot of reports that say trees do play a role in temperature control in and around the cities, but according to the U.S. Forest Service, that's too simplistic an answer.

Still, we do know that trees serve a variety of purposes in the cities. They do clean the air, provide sound buffers and reduce urban blight by adding beauty. In addition to helping clean urban air by removing carbon dioxide and releasing oxygen, they can reduce flooding by intercepting rainfall. Trees also freshen up the polluted atmosphere with their own fragrances. One cherry tree can perfume the air with 200,000 flowers — much better than smelling car exhaust!

Trees also bring urban residents closer to nature and help people feel they belong to a larger natural environment. Trees can help reduce stress levels and can even help people recuperate from illness faster. A 1994 study found that patients in a hospital whose windows offered a view of a wooded landscape got better faster and with less medicine than those who could only look out on a brick wall.

It's sometimes hard to define the difference between a city park and an urban forest. But one thing is clear: we tend to want different things from our urban forests than we do those in the "wild."

Our urban forests are often battlegrounds over space and facilities. There's always a conflict between those who want trees and those who want baseball fields and picnic areas. Also, recreational use of some urban parks and forests is virtually nonstop, which can irritate those who simply want to enjoy the peace of trees and birdsong. Even worse, many of our urban forests are the scene of social conflict. Homeless people sleep in parks. Some parks invite crime and vandalism. There is even the problem of "pet pollution."

These problems are exacerbated when, in times of tight budgets, we leave our parks to their own devices. I believe that is so wrong. The same care and attention we give to our state and national parks and forests should be given to those in the city. It is so important for the human psyche to be able to have at least some access to nature.

Urban forests are generally put into four categories: the suburban fringe, the suburbs, the city residential and the city center. American Forests recommends cities set a canopy cover goal of 40 percent overall — which comes out to about 20 large trees per acre. The central downtown area should aim for 15 percent coverage, with urban neighborhoods and fringe business areas going for 25 percent. Suburbs should be able to have a tree canopy of 50 percent.

While these goals might seem idealistic at best, the effort is underway. There are hundreds of civic and governmental agencies all designed to plant and protect trees in the city. They have great names, such as "Denver Digs Trees," "Forestry for Phoenix," and "Tree Folks" in Hartford, Connecticut.

Trees Atlanta is another such group. Since 1985, this organization has planted more than 14,000 large shade trees in downtown Atlanta along the main streets. To get instant shade and visual impact, the group plants large hardwoods – about 18 feet tall – as well as beautiful evergreen magnolias and hollies. Among the group's favorite hardwoods are willow oaks, legacy sugar maple, lacebark elm and village green zelkovas. Tree cover for Atlanta and the surrounding counties is only about 27 percent. But as the downtown trees planted by Trees Atlanta and other organizations grow, they'll increase the tree canopy in the hottest part of the city by 3 percent.

Urban planting, thanks to Trees Atlanta.

TREES ATLANTA

There are other success stories across the country, as well.

Milwaukee, Wisconsin, for example, has an acclaimed urban forest management program. In 1995, the city conducted an urban ecosystem analysis of its urban forests and concluded that the benefits of an urban forest extend into several areas of economic and social importance. First, its existing tree canopy cover of about 16 percent reduces storm water flow by up to 222 percent and provides the city an estimated $15.4 million in benefits. And second, the trees in Milwaukee also do their jobs as air filters. The city estimates the trees not only help lower air temperatures but also trap about 1,677 tons of carbon annually, saving about $1.5 million each year in pollution control requirements.

The citizens of Lexington, Kentucky, are also proud of their trees. Lexington's urban forester, David Swenk, developed a method for reforesting the floodplains in Fayette County, planting more than 35,000 native trees and creating a 77-acre riparian forest. A great success, "Reforest the Bluegrass" has turned into a yearly event with substantial backing from local sources and volunteers.

In Baltimore, a revitalization project merged the state's department of natural resources, the USDA Forest Service and ordinary citizens in an effort to plant trees along streets, streamsides and vacant lots. In addition, they organized to clean, monitor and restore riparian areas, and to foster environmental awareness among young people. Overall, Baltimore has a tree cover of 25 percent, with the suburban area averaging 31 percent.

Southern Dade County, Florida, still feels the effects of Hurricane Andrew, which left Miami and the surrounding county with a tree cover of only 15 percent. Three years later, the citizens passed a landscape ordinance that specified the need to plant trees where they will be most beneficial for energy conservation. New trees are quickly replacing the lost ones.

The stories of success in urban forestry go on and on, but failure and neglect also persist. The point is that each town, each city must recognize the beauty and the economic benefit of trees and strive to preserve and protect them.

As Bryce Nelson observed, "People who will not sustain trees will soon live in a world that will not sustain people."

CHAPTER TEN

⌒

STEWARDSHIP

"Stewardship: The conducting, supervising or managing of something; esp: the careful and responsible management of something entrusted to one's care."
~ Merriam Webster's Collegiate Dictionary

"You don't belong in the forest if you don't know how to give back to the forest," Kumu Hula Pua Kanahele, an expert on traditional Hawaiian culture, told a conference in Hawaii a few years back. So true.

What must we do to maintain the beauty and productivity of the forests for today and generations to come? It's a complicated problem. But how we go about achieving that aim involves an effort by all of us—tree farmers, loggers, forest companies, retail outlets, politicians environmentalists and most of all, consumers. In other words, each and every one of us. We must all act as good stewards to use, conserve, manage, and grow our forests.

Being a guardian of the forest means recognizing the value of forests in our everyday life. We need to judge our forests not just for the economic value of the resulting lumber, pulp, or other products, but on the overall contributions trees make—such as improving air quality, preventing erosion and providing pure beauty and recreational fun.

WHAT IS A SUSTAINABLE FOREST?

Although the term "managed sustainable forests" has a lot of different meanings and nuances, the concept of sustainability is what should be guiding us all. Generally speaking, sustainable management maintains the essential function of the complex forest ecosystems while allowing timber production. However, timber production is allowed only after several safeguards are in place, among them:

- The forest's values must be studied, fully understood and then maintained.
- The natural relationships of the forest, such as the interactions of the various ecosystems, should to a degree be copied and maintained.
- Harvesting must be done in such a way as to make minimal impact on the environment.
- No more timber should be harvested than what can be replaced by new growth, either through natural reforestation or by planting.

In a sustainable forest, timber is harvested in a way that meets the needs of the present while at the same time improving the long-term health and future productivity of the forest. The sustainability ethic integrates the reforestation, management, growing, nurturing and harvesting of trees for useful products while, at the same time, ensuring soil, air and water quality, wildlife and fish habitats, and the beauty of the land.

Like parents rearing children, those of us who oversee forests must protect them from bad outside influences such as pests, diseases and other damaging agents. We must recognize those forests and lands that are of special significance (archeological, cultural, historical, biological or geographical), and handle them in a manner that takes into account their uniqueness. Most importantly, we must continuously improve the practice of forest management and monitor, measure and report the performance of others in order to achieve the commitment to sustainability.

To this end, many studies are being done by colleges and universities as well as within the industry. Some studies are a collaboration of all. One such study is being done now on wood quality. A collaboration between the Warnell School of Forest Resources at the University of Georgia, Auburn University, North Carolina State, the University of Florida, Virgina Tech, and partly sponsored by some industry players as well as some private landowners, this study is a model of stewardship principals. While we currently have a great deal of information on *how* to grow trees faster using genetic technology, fertilization, use of herbicides to control competition, thinning methods and pruning, at present we don't know much about the effects these techniques have on *wood quality*. Factors such as specific gravity, wood density, strength, and fiber characteristics will be intensely studied under this co-operative program. The results of these tests will allow us to better understand how to use the wood products we are growing. It can also give us ideas for improving wood quality for the future, and will no doubt spur the creativity of those involved in wood science. These types of studies are so important for our future forests, as they seek to find accurate answers to many questions, resulting in a better understanding and use of the resource.

The idea of sustainable forests has been around for a long, long time. However, the term formally came into use in 1992 when the United Nations called an "earth summit" in Brazil to discuss strategies to promote sustainable forestry practices through management standards, professional associations and third-party certification. Since then, most of the developed world has embraced at least some of the practices of sustainability.

Part of the problem is that the idea of sustained forestry as a philosophy is more accepted than it is as a set of actual management practices. Nevertheless, with so many special interests at play, most of us want to practice good stewardship and sustainability—even if we don't all agree as to which road to take to get to the same goal.

The American Tree Farm System, for example, has adopted a set of standards which all 65,000 of its members [including Rose Lane and me] must follow. They include these 12 principles:

- Broaden the practice of sustainable forestry
- Ensure prompt reforestation
- Protect water quality
- Enhance wildlife habitat
- Minimize the visual impact of harvesting
- Protect special sites
- Contribute to biodiversity
- Continue to improve wood utilization
- Continue the prudent use of chemicals to ensure forest health
- Foster the practice of sustainable forestry on all forestlands
- Publicly report progress
- Provide opportunities for public involvement

Similarly, the Society of American Foresters adopted a code of ethics that demonstrates its respect for the land and its commitment to stewardship. It encourages members to advocate and practice land management consistent with ecologically sound principles. It also says that a member's knowledge and skills will be utilized for the benefit of

Logo of the American Tree Farm System.

society and that stewardship is the cornerstone of the forestry profession.

CERTIFICATION

Perhaps the biggest issue facing the lumber and forestry industries is the issue of certification. At its most basic level, certification is a way to verify that each piece of lumber sold has been harvested from a tree farm or forest that uses good management practices. In other words, the wood must come from those who "walk the walk" of the principles of sustainability.

A certified piece of wood is similar to organically produced food. On the food there is an emblem stating that the food was grown under certain and provable conditions. It's sort of like a warranty.

There are two main steps to certifying wood products. The first, forest management certification, involves an assessment of the on-site forest management practices and/or management systems against performance indicators of specified social, ecological and economic standards. Other names for this step are forest certification, forest management auditing or timber certification.

The next step, wood product certification, involves a "chain-of-custody" verification that tracks the wood harvested in certified forests through all stages of transport, processing and marketing to the finished product. Often called "forest product labeling," this step verifies that the timber was produced according to a particular set of good forest management standards.

These are the two basic approaches to certification. One, a more goal-oriented approach, is to verify whether a landowner has adopted quality management processes that are consistent with the goals of sustainability. The second is to measure specific characteristics related to the origins of the end product with performance indications, such as the economy or ecology.

In the environmental community, three basic principles keep cropping up in regard to wood certification. They are:

- Fully functioning ecosystems must be maintained both during and after timber cutting.
- Ecosystem functioning must be protected at all times and at all scales (stand level and landscape level).

- Forest-based communities must have fair and legal access to and benefit from the forest close to them.

As of this writing, there are several entities vying for position as authorities on forest certification (sometimes also called "Green Certification"). And at present, some of the major organizations that are involved can't agree as to the best course of action.

The Forest Stewardship Council (FSC), sponsored by the Mexico-based World Wildlife Fund, argues for its own independent evaluation system. It believes that the forest products industry is a complex web of interrelationships among producers, suppliers, manufacturers, wholesalers and customers, and, as a result, it is very hard to determine where the wood comes from and where it will end up. Therefore, it favors what it claims is an independent evaluation of a forest company and landowner's practices to keep that company and landowner on the straight and narrow path.

The council maintains that this is the only system which verifies claims from the forest all the way to the final product – "chain of custody" monitoring. When a customer purchases a wood product and sees the FSC logo, that customer is assured that the purchase supports sustainable forestry. A noble goal, and I'm sure they believe they're doing the right thing. But they have a "one size fits all" set of standards, and, in my opinion, it isn't fair to some parts of the world to make them adhere to those standards. What's more, the expenses involved with this organization are rather high, meaning that landowners have to pay a substantial fee to FSC to get their wood certified. Most tree farmers would certainly agree that since we already have enough tax expenses – not to mention our investment in land and management expenses, our costs due to losses from insects and disease, and so many other pay-outs – the thought of having to pay someone to somehow verify that we are indeed acting as good stewards is not very palatable.

Another group, the Certified Forest Products Council, based in Beaverton, Oregon, is a trade organization that not only supports third-party certification but has also presented a huge challenge to the entire forest industry. The council's president, David Ford, has said the industry has the opportunity to "transform itself from product manufacturer into service provider and our forests can be more than warehouses of raw material to be extracted."

The industry must be a steward of the forests, says Ford, so it can be "credited for delivering all those services that exist before trees are converted into products, including habitat, biodiversity, water cleansing and storage, carbon sequestration, oxygen generation, recreation and spiritual sanctuary."

In addition, a landowner group in Europe has emerged as a possible forest certification entity: the Pan European Forest Council, or PEFC. This group represents private landowners throughout Europe that have banded together to create their own set of standards for certification and sustainability. Finally, there are groups in Africa, Asia and other parts of the world, each of which represents the unique circumstances of those areas. Most of these organizations share the same basic principals of sustainability, but take into account their own particular situations. For instance, here in America, the American Forest and Paper Association created the Sustainable Forestry Initiative, or SFI, to deal with certification. The association believes in policing its own and has its own standards of sustainability. Their standards are similar to the FSC's, but without some of the more radical concepts and heavy expenses involved. The American Tree Farm System will soon release its latest set of standards for family-owned forests – developed and reviewed by an expert panel that included family owners, environmentalists, foresters and academics. ATF and SFI have already signed an agreement recognizing each other's certification standards. It is my hope that this agreement will pave the way for future similar agreements.

In my opinion we cannot have a "one size fits all" or "cookie cutter" policy for certification. Different parts of the world have different situations, requiring a more regional approach. What we do in the Southeast U.S. in forest management may not be the right approach for Europe or a region of Central America or New Zealand. And, of course, that works both ways. What is right for them is not necessarily right for us.

I believe that we need to form mutually recognized entities in various parts of the world that can work together to maintain worldwide sustainability through certification.

Some feel that certification and sustainability pit the western world, with its stable and wealthy economies, against Third World countries, such as Brazil and Costa Rica, that need all the revenue they can clear from their rain forests to feed families. Others believe that with more stringent harvesting methods, the cost of wood products would go up and demand would eventually go down, hurting tree farmers, retailers and forest companies.

In addition, it could be argued that certification is easier for the large landowners and corporate forest companies because they have the resources to absorb the costs of certification compliance while the small tree farmer does not. Along those same lines, since certification to a degree requires a solid knowledge of tree farming, science and ecology, it would certainly be more difficult for less educated and poorer farmers to learn and understand the various baseline requirements for certification. Certification could thus place a burden on the poorer, less sophisticated tree farmer.

By its very nature, certification acknowledges environmental limits and costs that will have repercussions across the board. It may set some standards and goals about yields that would lower the current or proposed productivity of some forests, but it could also conceivably allow for an increased harvest of other forests.

It is almost unprecedented that many environmental groups, such as the World Wildlife Fund, Greenpeace and the Natural Resources Defense Council, agree with businesses such as Home Depot and Assi Doman, one of Sweden's largest forest companies, that forest product certification—in some form or another—encourages the protection of the forests and is also a sound business practice. I challenge anyone to find big business and environmental groups on the same side of any other issue!

Let's take Atlanta-based Home Depot, which is the largest retailer of wood and wood products. In 1999, it pledged to stop selling wood products from environmentally sensitive areas. It also promised to increase products made with wood from certified Well-Managed Forests. That means that a supplier's wood must be tracked from the forest, through manufacturing, to the distribution at the Home Depot store.

Another company that recently agreed to certification is Centex, one of America's largest homebuilders. The company is now giving preference to vendors who subscribe to one of a range of certification programs. Lowe's, another well-known large retail chain, also has jumped on the certification bandwagon.

While all of these businesses are well-meaning, the truth is that to a large degree, the executives involved don't really know a lot about forest management, and therefore are sometimes misguided.

For instance, a Lowe's executive recently stated that the forests in the Southeast U.S. were "endangered." Nothing could be further from the truth! It is this kind of misleading statement that causes confusion and misunderstanding among the general public. If those involved would get into the field with the foresters, land managers and landowners, they would do themselves a great favor.

In my own personal view, there is a happy medium to be met in forest certification. I do believe we need to have strong standards, but I don't believe in the radical stance that some so-called environmentalists take. Let's face it, some of them would be happy if we never harvested another tree.

We have to find the proper balance, and to me, that's what it's all about.

On a positive note, research indicates that a majority of consumers are willing to pay a premium price for certified products, just as they do for organic produce. According to Catherine Mater, a well-known engineer and expert on the marketing of "green" products, more than 90 percent of wood product manufacturers stated a preference for certified lumber in their operations. On the consumer side, more than 70 percent said they wanted independent certification rather than government or industry certification, she said.

So You Want to Be an American Tree Farmer...

Although certification is a key element toward managing our forests, it is the job of tree farmers everywhere to grow the wood needed while still protecting our watersheds and wildlife habitat, conserving soil and providing recreation. Since 58 percent of the productive forests in the U.S. is owned by ordinary citizens, it is important to know that we can place our trust in these men and women. Indeed these 9.9 million forest landowners hold the key to what kind of forests future generations of Americans will enjoy.

To some, the concept of tree farming is silly. What's so hard about planting a tree and coming back 20 years later and cutting it down?

Well, believe me, it is not that simple. It takes years, even decades of careful and frequent maintenance of the trees and land to ensure a successful harvest.

Sound sustainable forestry begins with determining your objectives. Then you must understand what type of land you have, what species will do well on that land and in that climate, and what the long-term goals are. The next step is to develop a forest management plan, something a professional forester can often help you with by answering questions and making suggestions.

Of course, there are many fine schools and universities that teach the principles of sound forestry. Other sources of good forestry practices include the landowner assistance programs available through some industry participants (like Georgia Pacific, Weyerhaeuser, and others), information from state forestry associations and commissions, landowner-based groups (Forest Landowners Association, American Tree Farm System and others), state extension services and even correspondence courses. I wrote the plan for our tree farm after completing a correspondence course offered by the Forest Landowner's Association and the Extension Service of the University of Georgia in 1985. I was working at the time with the Fabulous Thunderbirds, a rhythm and blues band from Texas, and the course was mostly completed in the back of the tour bus!

Regardless of where or how you do it, a good tree farmer has a plan. To qualify for the American Tree Farm System designation—their logo is "Wood, Water, Wildlife and Recreation"—a tree farmer must meet several criteria. Among them are that the woodlands must be 10 or more acres and there must be an implemented plan that accounts for water quality, wildlife habitat and solid conservation as well as production of forest products. Included in the plan must be provisions to protect the land from wildfire, insects, disease and destructive grazing.

Once these standards are met, a free inspection of woodlands can be arranged through a State Tree Farm Committee. More than 6,000 foresters volunteer their time in order to conduct these inspections. In order to ensure that the landowners are continuing to meet the rigorous forestry certification criteria, every tree farm is reinspected every five years.

Certified tree farmers receive a certificate and a sign that indicates that excellent forestry is practiced there. Tree farmers like myself share the satisfaction that comes from managing their land to the highest standards of good stewardship as well as the resulting peer recognition that comes from this commitment.

Each year tree farmers from around the country compete for the honor of being named state, regional or national Tree Farmer of the Year. Rose Lane and I have twice been honored as Georgia Tree Farmers of the Year, and in 1999, we captured the national honor. Looking back at all of the accomplishments in my life, being named the National Outstanding Tree Farmer of the Year is just as good a feeling as when I've received a gold or platinum record or been on a recording that has won a Grammy Award.

Maybe even better.

CHALLENGES OF TREE FARMING

But like the rest of America's farmers, tree farmers face a number of challenges trying to make a living. A committed tree farmer must be aware of and involved in these issues that impact the care, management and health of our forests.

Private property rights, one of the fundamental issues in this country, is such an area. The freedom to own and use private property without arbitrary government interference is one of the basic rights of all Americans. However, lately our country has witnessed an explosion of federal regulation that has jeopardized the private ownership of property, with the loss of individual freedom.

Governmental regulations—whether state, local or federal—can impact tree farmers in a number of ways, including:

- Harvesting fees
- Requirements for public hearings and permits prior to harvesting
- Excessive buffer requirements
- Requirements exceeding state-mandated best-management practices
- Prohibitions on prescribed burning
- Outright prohibitions on timbering

Once again, the irony of these misguided requirements is that they are often imposed with the intention of saving trees. But in many cases, the actual result is that they can cause landowners to sell their land for development because their timber no longer has any value. This is one of the reasons we have seen the explosion of "Urban Sprawl" here in the United States in recent years. If there are too many restrictions on forest management, the logical choice is to sell out to a developer who is offering a high price for the land, resulting in the attitude of "take the money and run."

Throughout the country, states have taken proactive steps to address the problems associated with excessive local regulation of silviculture (i.e., tree farming or forestry) practices. These are generally referred to as private property rights initiatives or right-to-practice forestry laws. Frankly, across the country, these laws have met with mixed success. Some have been successful; others did not accomplish the goal or didn't go far enough.

TAXES

As volatile as the certification issue is among tree farmers, so is the issue of taxes. Local governments often rely on property taxes as one of their main sources of income. As a result of this dependence, and the increasing pressures placed on property owners, tree farmers have become increasingly sensitive to the many demands placed upon them to shoulder local government and educational funding. The laws facing tree farmers today make it even more difficult to pay taxes and pass the land on to their heirs.

For example, if a natural disaster destroys a crop like corn or oranges, there are a number of places to go for relief. A farmer could get clean-up help through the Emergency Conservation Program. Not so for a tree farmer. In the infinite wisdom of some of our agricultural governmental agencies, timber is not really a crop. And since a tree farmer, in the eyes of the government, doesn't have an annual crop, he is not considered on par with other farmers and therefore receives no assistance.

How about a Catch 22? Fine, if some of the agricultural agencies won't help the tree farmer in times of disaster, how about another outlet—the Small Business Administration? Nope. The SBA doesn't give loans to agricultural enterprises and the SBA considers tree farmers to be farmers.

Let's run that one again. Some federal agencies won't give assistance to tree farmers because they're not farmers, and some won't give it to them because they are!

It gets even worse.

Again, a tree farmer who experienced a loss—say, a drought or fire—could reasonably expect to deduct that loss from his or her income taxes. Wrong again! Instead of allowing a deductible equal to the loss, the IRS limits the deduction to the cost basis of the timber less any compensation—like revenue from a salvage sale.

Basically, the IRS says a deduction can't be anymore than the cost of establishing the damaged stand of trees adjusted for any income from salvage. Whatever increase in value a tree farmer would have realized because of tree growth and increase in timber prices is lost—and not deductible. Moreover, losses due to insects, diseases or drought are not considered casualty losses and are not deductible at all.

The IRS, you see, doesn't recognize that trees are a commodity—one that grows each year and generally increases in value annually. Most tree farmers don't sell their growth each year; rather they allow the trees to grow over several or many years. If they suffer a casualty loss while growing, that marketable quantity is not acknowledged.

Another area where tree farmers face archaic laws is with inheritance taxes. My wife Rose Lane and I have a personal experience in this.

When she inherited the "home place" from her grandmother back in 1981, things were a lot different than they are now. The exemption for estate taxes was $300,000, and the interest rates were about 20 percent.

We had tried to do some estate tax planning before Miss Julia (Rose Lane's grandmother) passed away. We began buying some land to get it out of the estate and Miss Julia began to "gift" some of the land to family members, which the law allows. However, she passed away after the second year of this estate planning, and the government said that we made these legal moves "in contemplation of death" and disallowed our planning. It was too little, too late.

Not only did we face the grim tax reaper, but we had paid an accountant and lawyers a substantial sum for the "estate planning" work. After assessing the situation, we realized that we were in trouble. We had nowhere near the amount of money to pay the initial tax bill, which was mostly just interest due. We were afraid that if we went out and borrowed the money, especially with the extremely high interest rates at the time, we might not be able to pay it back.

We discussed this with the family, as Rose Lane's brother Alton was to receive a similar amount of land from Miss Julia and was in the same financial situation.

Some years earlier, Rose Lane and Alton's father had passed away and left them about 300 acres of land in a different county, about 60 or so miles away. As much as it hurt to do so, the only way to make the payment due to the IRS was to sell this 300-acre tract. It was land that had been passed down for many generations. It was like selling a part of our soul, especially for Rose Lane and Alton, but there was simply no other alternative.

So the land was put on the market and sold before too long, giving us the necessary funds to make the first payment. Of course, there was a hefty tax bill on the gain from that land sale, so we had to satisfy the IRS on our personal returns for that as well.

But that was only the beginning! We had completed the estate tax return as best and as honestly as we could, and made the initial payment. We were under a rule that allows for some relief to farm estates, which essentially gave us 15 years to pay off the remaining funds. Still, every year—for 15 years—we had to come up with a substantial amount of money, plus interest, to pay the IRS. In order to make these payments we had to periodically sell some of our timber. Even this couldn't cover all the debt. Thank goodness I had my musical career, as much of the income from my touring and recording during those years went to make up the difference. I don't want to even think about what we would have done if we had not had a "second job."

The IRS has seven years to audit estate tax returns, and of course, we got audited at the end of the seventh year. We had to hire a lawyer (another big bill) and go to battle once again. Finally, after a great deal of negotiation, the estate was settled—which, as we all know, means that we owed the IRS even more money. Not only did we owe them the money, according to the IRS' reckoning, but the interest as well, which at that time was still in double digits.

When all was said and done, we paid the IRS nearly half a million dollars in estate taxes and interest for the land we inherited. So you can understand why I tell people now that we didn't "inherit" anything. The U.S. government inherited our land, and we had to buy it back from them!

Our story is not unique. We readily admit that we are among the lucky ones who were able to come up with the money to keep our land, even if we had to sell some of it in order to keep the rest. Many American families have to sell most or all of their land to satisfy their estate tax bills. The end result is the loss of family farms and the American dream.

Only six months after Miss Julia's death, Congress and then-President Reagan doubled the exemption to make it $600,000. At this writing the exemption is $1.0 million and is scheduled to increase to $3.5 million by 2009. The maximum rate of federal estate tax is also scheduled to decline from 50% in 2002 to 45% in 2009 and then is scheduled to be eliminated altogether in 2010. However, this phase-out of the estate tax expires after December 31, 2010. Unless Congress acts to make the estate tax repeal permanent or take other action, the federal estate tax exemption will again decline to $1.0 million and the tax rate will rise to as high as 60%. So unless Congress acts, estate taxes will continue to be a major issue for forest landowners in just a few short years.

So as you can see, stewardship of our forests is a complicated issue. It's not as easy as some think, given all the twists and turns to our laws, regulations and programs here in America. Still, the principals of stewardship should be—and in my opinion for the most part are—the guiding light of those that own forestland and work in the forests in our country.

As I travel around the world, my message is a simple one. Use the forests wisely. Don't abuse them. Stewardship should be practiced every day by those of us who rely on trees for our living and for those of us who rely on trees to make our living better.

Let's do right by the land and what is on and under it.

CHAPTER ELEVEN

WHERE ARE WE NOW?

"In the woods we return to reason and faith."
~ Ralph Waldo Emerson

When I talk to people about our forests, the main questions I always hear are these:

"Aren't we cutting down all of our forestland?"

"Don't we have much less now than we did just a few decades ago?"

"Won't we run out of trees soon?"

The answers, thank heaven, are balanced heavily on the positive side. Ever since sound forest management practices became widely used, the state of our forests and their current and future health have been an important part of the American psyche—and rightly so. We have fought to protect them as we use their many gifts. Forests helped build this country, and they will help build its future. To me, this is the most exciting time for our forests. When I think back about how close this country came to losing its forests and how healthy and vibrant they are today, I feel so thankful.

As we enter the new century, American forests cover about one-third of the country—almost 749 million acres. That's mind-boggling! When the earliest pioneers came, there were about one billion acres of forestland. So even with all of our development, we still have close to 70 percent of that original amount. Now, a naysayer could see that as losing 30 percent of our forests. But I think it's remarkable that a country our size, with a population of more than 280 million and with all of our urban sprawl, has kept 70 percent. We've accommodated the entire growth of this great nation and still have 70 percent of our forests!

What's more, our trees have never been in better hands. Not only are we practicing good forest-management techniques, but the new technology available will help us and Mother Nature to do an even better job in protecting and continuing the health and diversity of the forests.

Just like taking a person's temperature or blood pressure, there are scientific ways to measure the health of the forests and to tell whether we have enough trees to meet our needs. The University of Michigan's School of Natural Resources and Environment, in cooperation with the U.S. Department of Agriculture Forest Service, recently did an exhaustive audit of our forests, and the results are something to cheer about.

In 1690, the Mid Atlantic states (Ohio, Pennsylvania, West Virginia, Maryland, Delaware and New Jersey) had 80 million acres of forests and few people. By 1890, there were 24 million acres of forests and 12 million people. In 1990, that figure is an astonishing 40 million acres of forestland existing peacefully with more than 36 million people.

The rest of the country can tell similar stories. In 1850, only 35 percent of Vermont was forested. Today, that figure is 80 percent. Upstate New York has three times the population it had 150 years ago, but it has three times as much forest as it had back then.

Another great example is Idaho where more than 18 million new trees a year are planted by hand. That averages out to 18 trees for every man, woman and child in the state. Don't forget that Mother Nature adds millions of new trees on her own each year too. Net growth of trees in Idaho is two and one-half times what net tree removals are annually.

LONGLEAF PINES ARE COMING BACK.

We are also gathering our forces to try to help tree species that have been dying off. A good example of this is the longleaf pine. Of all the Southern pines, many consider the longleaf pine the most valuable in terms of quality of wood products, the most aesthetically pleasing and the most resistant to insects, disease and fires.

Before the European settlers came, extensive stands of longleaf pine ranged from east Texas through the lower coastal plain to Virginia. At that time, about 60 million acres of the longleaf pine ecosystem existed. Today, only about three million acres exist. North Carolina was once called the "land of the longleaf pine," with about one-third of the state—11 million acres— covered by the trees. Today, only about 225,000 acres, mostly in the eastern part, remain. The forests were largely decimated by the early 1990s due to land clearing and fire suppression. That's right ... suppression. Those trees need frequent fires. Without fires, the natural or planted seedlings may remain stuck in the early "grass stage" for years. They die before their stems can grow and turn into trees.

In the past 80 years or so, the loblolly and slash pine have become the pine trees of choice in the South. But the longleaf pine is not forgotten. Over the past three years, the park service has started habitat restoration efforts on more than 1,300 acres in Georgia, Alabama, Florida, North Carolina and South Carolina. Government assistance programs are also in place to help private landowners re-introduce longleaf on their lands here in the South.

Of course, with the decline of the longleaf pine came the loss of other plants and animals that counted on the longleaf pine for food and shelter. In fact, more than 30 plant and animal species, including the red-cockaded woodpecker and the gopher tortoise, are now threatened. But there is a concerted effort to overcome the damage man inflicted on the longleaf pine stands.

Yes, man helped create the problem, but now we are helping solve it.

WHO'S IN CHARGE OF THE TREES?

Each year about 2 percent of our timber is cut and a slightly larger amount is regenerated.

Federal, state and local governments own about 45 percent or about 334 million acres of forest. Of that land, about 23 percent is in "strictly protected" areas, primarily national parks and wilderness areas where timber can never be harvested. In a geographical breakdown, about 12 million acres (or 3 percent) of all the trees in the eastern U.S. are under the strictly protected designation; 65 million acres (or 18 percent) are in the western U.S., including Alaska.

The U.S. Forest Services manages some 192 million acres of national forests. Unlike the trees in our national park system, these lands allow for multiple uses—recreation, wildlife conservation and harvesting for lumber and other forest products. Of those 192 million acres, about 77 percent is forested, and 35 percent is 'technically' available for planned timber harvests. I say 'technically' because much of this timberland is further subjected to habitat or roadless conservation restrictions. Only about one-tenth of one percent of the trees on national forest timberland is cut in any given year.

One recent, well-publicized controversy has been over the cutting of old-growth trees in our national forests. Old-growth trees are a feature of late-successional forests and are in the mature stages of their lives. In the Pacific Northwest, the Forest Service manages about 24 million acres and about 35% of that is late-successional forest with old-growth trees. The Northwest Forest Plan implemented by President Clinton is intended to protect and restore the mature forests in the region.

The forest products companies own about 9 percent of our forests, or about 66 million acres. Of the privately held land—either owned by corporations or families—about 39 percent is used for timber production or land investment purposes. About 18 percent is part of a private farm or residence, and another 17 percent is used for recreation or enjoyment purposes.

SAVING THE FORESTS THROUGH TECHNOLOGY

In the summer of 1995, I was touring Europe with the Rolling Stones. Prior to the tour, I had asked some friends at the University of Georgia if they had any contacts in Europe—folks who owned forestland or were otherwise involved in forestry that I might call and maybe spend time with while I was there. I was given the names of several people, amongst them Prince Albrecht Oettingen and his wife, Angela, who lived in the Bavarian region of Germany.

The Oettingens have a long history of managing their forestlands there. I mean a long history ... like centuries! As it turned out, they were both music fans and Angela was a long-time Stones fan. They came to our concert in Munich, and graciously invited me to come stay with them for a night and visit their forests.

While driving in the car to their place, Albrecht played a

trick on me. We were discussing forestry in general, and he told me of an experiment that had taken place years before in Germany. They had taken similar tracts of land of equal acreage and managed one intensively. The other was left to the whims of Mother Nature. The experiment had a focus on forestry and avian species, but also had data pertaining to all species of flora and fauna within the stands.

"So which one do you think had the most diversity of flora and fauna?" he asked. To me, the quick and obvious answer was that the natural, unmanipulated one, had the most.

"AHHH! Wrong!" he exclaimed. "The managed forest had much more diversity than the 'natural' one." I asked Albrecht to back this up with proof, and he was glad to do so. I soon received in the mail a translation of the results of the study: "Biological Conservation Through Diversity," by Professor Paul Muller, Director of the Institute of Biogeography and Speaker of the Center for Environmental Sciences, University des Saarelandes, Germany. Take my word for it, this study was extensive and convincing.

BUILDING 'BETTER TREES'

As we work together to make sure our trees are healthy and vibrant, we cannot overlook the miracles of science as a partner in this effort. One of the most significant developments that has helped the trees is the introduction of biotechnology—the study of genes—in forest management.

Gene manipulation is nothing new. New species of roses are made by taking the cuttings from two different species and putting them together to grow a new variety. When most of us learned this in school, it was called "cross-breeding." Now it's become much more complicated; it's called gene manipulation and genetic engineering.

On an even simpler basis, survival of the fittest is really a contest with the best genes winning. The plant or animal that survives and passes on its genes also gives its offspring whatever that special quality was—extra speed, intelligence, sturdiness—that allowed it to adapt more successfully to its environment. Over generations, that extra-strong feature takes hold.

Scientists today are giving nature a helping hand. Scientists isolate specific genes and transfer them from one organism to another. In some cases, the genes go from one plant species to another. In other cases, bacterial and animal genes are transferred into plants. The transfer of a bacterial gene into plants, for instance, can give them resistance to herbicides, making weed control easier and more efficient.

Scientists have different goals. Some want to create trees that are resistant to some insects or disease. Others want to speed up the maturity process so trees can be harvested faster.

Let's take the notion of genetically altering trees so they would not be so attractive to insects. Five species of insects defoliate about three percent of all U.S. forests. That's 21 million acres, an awful lot for a bunch of bugs to eat and kill. All except the gypsy moth are native. A new insect, the Asian long-horned beetle, has now been detected in both native trees and in imported packing materials in warehouses. Forest managers believe this beetle has the potential to severely damage maple and other popular trees.

Just think of all the good that can come out of making the trees more resistant to those insects – maybe by putting a gene in the tree that emits an odor or taste that the bugs no longer find pleasant.

Disease is another area where biotechnology could play a role. Researchers today are conducting different gene therapy trials to see if they can make people less susceptible to diseases such as cancer. It's the same with trees.

About 6 percent of the southern forests—13 million acres—is destroyed annually by fusiform rust, a disease. The dwarf-mistletoe, a parasitic plant, is responsible for the deaths of about 13 percent of the trees in the western forests—about 29 million acres.

Imagine the millions of trees that could be saved if we could help the trees fight their enemies and be less susceptible to disease. It's been estimated that by 2050, there will be a 40 percent increase in the world's demand for wood fiber. Not losing so many trees needlessly would go a long way to meet the demand.

Nearly every major forest company and most major universities are involved in gene therapy and manipulation. The Oregon State University Tree Genetic Engineering Research Cooperative has engineered hybrid poplars to resist the herbicide glyphosate (Roundup) and produce insecticidal Bt toxins. The program has also produced transgenetic hybrid poplars in the hopes of controlling a serious leaf-eating pest, the cottonwood leaf beetle.

Scientists in Australia have identified genes that form wood cells in eucalyptus in the hopes of creating trees with longer and thicker cells more suitable for paper making. If successful, it is thought that the growth time could be reduced to perhaps as little as eight years from 20 years.

While much of the genomic research has focused on producing trees for commercial purposes, there is also a concerted effort underway to help trees produce fruit quicker, again to meet the demands of a growing population. Agriculture research scientists have genetically engineered the forest dwarf pear trees. These trees, developed by inserting a gene originally isolated from a bacterium, are now growing in greenhouses and should be bearing fruit in a few years. In addition to being more productive, dwarf fruit trees allow high-density plantings of smaller trees. What this boils down to is smaller trees on less land producing more fruit! Win, win, win!

The once dominant American Chestnut tree in eastern forests has all but been wiped out by an introduced blight. Genetic research might hold the key to restoring this majestic species back into the forested landscape. Mighty oak trees too might be made inhospitable to the voracious gypsy moth.

All this biotechnology—some call it playing God—is in the very early stages. There are many who bring up valid questions about biotechnology. Some worry about long-term repercussions on the trees and the entire ecosystem. Others are concerned about the natural make-up of a forest—the plants, trees, grasses and animals—and how they will be affected by trees that came from the laboratory. Again, at a primitive level man has been manipulating genes for years, so I personally don't believe in any gloom-and-doom messages.

Current studies indicate that biodiversity of a landscape can actually be improved with a combination of plantings of genetically modified trees and controlled harvests of natural trees. In New Zealand, for example, plantation forests have demonstrated a wider range of diversity of both plant and animal life than some areas of native vegetation.

For all these reasons I'm excited about the future of our forests. Despite the increasing demand that will be placed upon them, the forests will remain strong and vibrant thanks to strong sustainability techniques, sound management and stewardship, and the wonders of science.

CHAPTER TWELVE

WHERE ARE WE GOING?

"Each generation takes the Earth as trustees. We ought to bequeath to posterity as many forests and orchards as we have exhausted and consumed."
~ J. Sterling Morton

Throughout my life, I've spent a lot of time talking to people – musicians, reporters, tree farmers, athletes, politicians, business tycoons or just plain folks – and it's always amazed me how people can look at the same set of facts and come up with two completely different interpretations.

In music, if you sell three million records, well, you've got a big hit. But if your next record sells two million, some will view it as a loser. It's the same with trees. The forestry industry could look at statistics reflecting the health of our forests and future projections and see a bright and rosy future. But an environmental organization might look at the same information and see disaster.

Like most things, I'm sure the truth is somewhere in between.

But what I know for sure is that we must come to some understanding about our timber resources. We need them for aesthetic reasons, recreation and conservation—but we also need them for our use. So whatever your view about forests and timber lands, we have got to take some cold hard looks at what we are doing and what we are planning for the future regarding the forest. We'd best pay close attention to what's going on, and we'd better get a balanced plan in place.

I've read many of the books about our forests and have talked to many of the experts. I think at present, we're looking pretty darn good. I think that we're still in good shape for the 21st century. We've somehow managed to keep our forests going through periods of tremendous growth, development, and timber consumption, and I know we can keep it up. But we all need to come together for the greater good.

Our forests are getting more attention and scrutiny than ever before. Some of that comes with the news and images of the horrible fires in 1999 and 2000 that destroyed millions of acres of forestland. But most of the attention these days, I believe, comes from a growing appreciation of our forests and the responsibilities we have to them. There's probably as much interest—and call for action—today as there was when the national forest system was being set up decades ago.

When talking about the future of our forests, we're really discussing two different issues: the future of our national forests and the future of our privately owned forests. We'll try to address the issues facing both parts of this equation.

Our national forests are managed by the U.S. Forest Service, which is in charge not only of the timber within them, but also of overseeing the safety of more than 3,000 wildlife and fish species and 10,000 plant species that live in our national forests. The government's budget is decreasing and our national forests are being scrutinized more than ever before. There are controversies about building roads through the forests, fire management and even logging on the lands.

The American forest products industry has a long and valued history of serving the American people. For most of

America's history, wood was practically our only fuel. Forests were the economic foundation of our nation. However, today that goal has changed. "Ecological sustainability" is at the top of the list concerning how we want the Forest Service to manage our forests. Now more than ever, the Forest Service faces the challenge of balancing the removal of forest products and maintaining a healthy ecosystem.

Many of today's citizens increasingly question the use of our national forests as sources of wood fiber or minerals. Public opinion has now shifted so that the rights of the Northern spotted owl, for instance, are viewed as being just as important as those of the loggers wanting to remove trees from public lands. Frankly, maybe even more so.

The American public has more than a passing interest in our national forests. More than 60 million Americans get their drinking water from watersheds that originate in our national forests and grasslands. Our national forests also provide 80 percent of the habitat in the lower 48 states for elk, mountain goat and bighorn sheep. They maintain 28 million acres of wild turkey habitat and half of the country's blue-ribbon streams.

"Ecological integrity," the new buzzword, means that the viability of key species and the habitat that those species require should be maintained almost at all costs. People today are strongly suggesting, if not demanding, that we focus less on what we take from the land and more on what we leave behind.

As part of that concern, there are loud cries to halt all logging on federal lands. In one of his last moves as chief executive, former President Bill Clinton announced a ban on construction of new roads and new commercial logging activities in almost 60 million acres of roadless terrain in the national forests. The action basically will halt any major expansion of logging in our national forests. The protected land, much of it in the West and Alaska, is about one-third of all the land in the national forests and more than the size of all the national parks combined. Included are about nine million acres of the Tongass National Forest in Alaska, which is the largest U.S. temperate rain forest.

While most environmental groups hail the order as one of the biggest conservation achievements in the history of the country, others, including those in the Forest Service, worry that the action will have negative effects, such as making it harder to fight wildfires and outbreaks of disease or insects. Loggers, naturally, are concerned about the repercussions on their business.

The U.S. government has been in the timber business for more than 100 years. Since 1899, the Forest Service and Bureau of Land management have sold more than 456 billion board of feet of timber, valued at about $20 billion.

Recently, however, logging has been on the decrease on federal lands. Timber sales in 2002 were $150 million, down substantially from $1.2 billion in 1992. In recent years, timber sales of less than two billion board feet have been a small fraction of the 12 billion a year sales prevalent in the 1980s. Clearcuts dropped from 163,00 acres a year to less than 23,000 as the type of timber sales changed.

In 1998 Forest Service Chief Mike Dombeck addressed the controversy.

"The primary purpose for most sales was to help meet the nation's demand for wood," Dombeck wrote. "Today, more and more sales are being designed to help attain various stewardship objectives that are best achieved through harvest. These objectives include thinning dense forest stands to restore historic ecological conditions, reducing excessive forest fuels and creating desired wildlife habitation."

In fact, Dombeck said that in 1993 the proportion of total harvest volume being removed for timber commodity purposes had fallen from 71 percent to 52 percent, while the proportion being removed for forest stewardship had grown from 23 percent to 40 percent. Part of the argument to reduce logging is economic. A recent assessment by the General Accounting Office claims that about $1 billion a year is used to subsidize logging in this country.

Others take a different direction, arguing that conserving national forests produces $30 for every dollar lost by the logging industry. In fact, the Forest Service predicted that in 2000, recreation, hunting and fishing in national forests would contribute 38 times more income to the nation's economy than logging, and would create 31 times more jobs. The Service estimated that in 2000, national forest lands would generate $110.7 billion from recreation, compared to $3.5 billion from timber harvest. These claims were subsequently criticized as based on a flawed and biased economic analysis, an indication of just how controversial the national forest timber program has been.

In 2001, 214 million people visited our national forests. They enjoyed the 9,126 miles of national scenic byways, and fished and canoed on our 4,418 miles of national wild and scenic rivers. Or maybe they hiked on our 133,087 miles or trails and camped in the 4,300 campsites. Whatever they did, they came to our national parks for enjoyment.

Interestingly, while the Forest Service must annually prove to Congress that its management of the forests provides maximum social and economic benefits for the least cost, its annual budget request has never included an analysis of the costs and benefits of the logging program. As increased charges of corporate welfare swirl around, the financial soundness of the logging practices will eventually be more scrutinized.

For the last several years, bipartisan proposals to phase out all commercial timber harvests in national forests and other federal lands have come before Congress. The latest large push occurred in 1997 with the National Forest Protection and

Restoration Act, which was submitted by Congressman Jim Leach, a Republican from Iowa, and Congresswoman Cynthia McKinney, a Democrat from Georgia.

The bill would have ended the federal timber sale program, protected all roadless areas from logging by canceling existing timber sales, prohibited all new timber sales and phased out all existing timber sales within two years and redirected logging subsidies to provide training for dislocated timber workers.

Congressman Leach at the time commented that "at first blush, some might think ending logging on national forests is environmental extremism, but in fact, it is common sense. The U.S. government is the only property owner I know which in effect pays private parties to deplete its resources."

Now with all this controversy, I don't personally support a zero-cut policy on our federal lands. I do believe we need to be smarter about it. I'm not sure our policy of timber quotas still works. Maybe we should start planning based on desired future conditions rather than quantities of board feet. There are ways of using timber harvest as a tool for achieving healthy watersheds and ecosystems, and I must say that I still support in part the original idea of the National Forests, which was, to an extent, to provide us with the resource of wood that we need. If we pursue that policy, we create opportunities in the forest products industry and in communities that depend on forest-related jobs.

President George W. Bush, Undersecretary of Agriculture Mark Rey, and the new chief of the Forest Service, Dale Bosworth, are taking a different approach. They want to protect roadless areas also, but believe that the Clinton-era rules closed the doors on management options necessary to improve or restore forest conditions. The complexity of environmental laws and regulations has prevented too many worthwhile projects from getting started or completed. Some 73 million acres of national forests and grasslands are at risk from catastrophic fires, and about 33 million acres are also at risk from insect and disease infestation. To address these problems, President Bush launched the *Healthy Forest Initiative (HFI)*. The HFI is intended to streamline the process of getting projects planned and implemented, especially near the wildland-urban interface.

Our national forests are also facing other threats. Here in the South in 2000, Tennessee saw one of the worst-ever outbreaks of Southern Pine Beetles and lost thousands of acres of what were healthy pine forests. The Forest Service believes that 24 million acres are at risk of excessive mortality over the next 15 years due to insect and disease outbreaks. For example, the gypsy moth, which is pervasive in the Northeast, could spread throughout much of the South and Midwest in the next 30 years. Fortunately, through survey and management practices, the Forest Service expects to slow the spread by up to 60 percent.

Forest fires are nothing new. Many start naturally when lightning strikes a tree. Most begin with carelessness, and a small number are started by professionals doing controlled burns that get out of hand. Unfortunately, that is exactly what happened in 2000 when more than 7.4 million acres of timberland burned uncontrollably, a record year. On average during the past ten years, nearly 80,000 wild fires destroyed 4.2 million acres each year, according to the National Interagency Fire Center. In 2002 there were more than 73,000 blazes, and nearly 7.2 million acres of forestland were scorched. Economic losses were more than $10 billion.

In fact, controlled burns are actually a very good way to *prevent* forest fires. Prescribed burns clear the clutter on the ground that can catch fire quickly and spread it, along with benefiting the trees and wildlife. A fire's heat is the only thing that will open the cones of the great redwoods so the seeds can escape and germinate. Young longleaf pine also depend largely upon fire to survive. There are also fire-dependent bird species, such as the endangered scrub jay, which can survive and prosper when fire clears the oak scrub. In the resulting new growth, the scrub jay can find the insects that compose its principal diet.

Before a professional starts a prescribed burn, it is necessary to get atmospheric data. The Haines Index gauges the potential for a forest fire to grow and spread. It takes into account the moisture content of the air at 10,000 feet and the stability of the layer of air between 10,000 and 18,000. On a scale of two to six, the index rates the danger of a fire in terms of the potential for those atmospheric conditions to draw flames into the sky and spread burning embers to other places.

In addition, it is vital to ensure there are enough personnel around to manage the fire or to fight it if it gets out of control and becomes a wildfire. That has been increasingly difficult for federal agencies that have experienced budget and personnel cutbacks.

The National Forest System estimated that there was a 5.8 percent decrease in firefighters nationwide from 8,160 workers in 1999 to 7,691 in 2000. In addition, the reduction of seasonal workers also had an impact on the number of forest fires in 2000. These crews often cleared trails and prepared prescribed burn areas. Without their work, the fires spread quicker.

The fires of 2000 were so devastating that Washington took notice and opened the bank. The Forest Service and the Department of the Interior released the funds to hire about 350 positions to support the National Fire Plan. This funding will bring the fire-fighting capability to full strength, which is great news. In 2001, the Forest Service hired more than 17,600 fire employees, a substantial increase, but still short of their goal of over 19,000.

Private landowners are facing many of the same challenges as the Forest Service. Large timber companies and large landowners are finding their practices under scrutiny from shareholders, customers and employees. Business as usual seems to be coming to an end.

In fact, proposed reforms of private logging can come from a variety of sources. The Pacific Coast Federation of Fishermen's Associations (PCFFA) want reforms in logging practices, as they claim it affects their fishing industry. To them, forestry is a fish issue. Salmon fishing and logging are the two most lucrative forest-dependent industries on the West Coast. Sediment washed down from poorly managed forests can harm or destroy estuaries, affect crab and shrimp nurseries, and hurt salmon production.

PCFFA says that what salmon need most is old-growth forests. They claim that because there are no large shade trees near stream banks, what the salmon are finding in some instances are river systems that are full of sediment or chemical pollutants or that are too hot to support healthy salmon populations. These fishermen see their livelihoods threatened by current and past forestry practices. They will be just one of many vocal groups getting their point of view across about logging.

States like California are seeking to dictate how private forest lands can be managed. Such plans supposedly ensure that each native commercial species be retained in order to maintain and improve tree species diversity, genetic material and seed production. In addition, it is being mandated that the best phenotypes available in the pre-harvest stand be maintained in order to give the best genes a chance to populate. Other considerations include rules for wildlife habitats, consideration of the cumulative impact on a stand due to logging, and watercourse and lake protection zone rules.

But in some cases, all of this regulation causes more problems than solutions. It can become too much of a burden on private landowners to meet all of the regulations, not to mention the expense, and therefore cause them to sell out to developers in order to make a profit. Again, we have to find a balance to make it work out.

In the South, where 90% of the forests are privately owned, people are also voicing concerns about timber harvesting. They see vast pine plantations and new wood-using mills, and associate them with the loss of natural landscapes. Public concern has been so great that the Forest Service led a major interagency assessment of trends and conditions of southern forests. What they found was not that surprising to those of us who live in the South. While plantations are replacing many natural pine stands, and the timber industry is expanding to meet growing demand, the Assessment concluded that population growth and rapid urbanization are the most significant forces of change in the region. The study predicted that about 31 million acres of southern forests will be urbanized or developed between 1992 and 2040. What this means is that forests are increasingly being influenced by the controversies created by the way different people see our forests.

I think we all must wake up and see that things are changing. We need to recognize what the forest means to us and address its future now instead of later. There is little margin for error. We must face the realities, adapt and carry on. If we blow it, if we miscalculate or fail to pay attention, then we will be facing serious problems. We must figure out how to meet timber supply needs in an ecologically sensitive manner, and we must educate America on the realities.

Americans want three things from their forests: a sustainable wood supply, jobs in rural communities, and values associated with healthy forests and healthy ecosystems, such as clean water and recreation. We need to deliver all three. We must never forget that each is as important as the other. We can do it.

And hopefully, we will.

CHAPTER THIRTEEN

⌒

FUTURE FORESTS

"Oh God, Chuck's talking about trees again!"
~ Keith Richards

I've taken a lot of good-natured kidding from my rock 'n' roll buddies about my other love — tree farming. When I first started out, my life at Charlane to them was a source of amusement and some bewilderment. Few could understand why I wouldn't want to live in L.A., New York, Nashville or even Atlanta in order to be in the thick of the music scene. No one really believed I lived in rural Georgia on a tree farm.

But, as we've all grown older – or, in many cases, simply survived — my fellow musicians and artists have come to appreciate the life I have when I'm not on the road. They may not understand it all, but they do understand something about the need to be good stewards of the land, as well as my personal need for a quiet respite from the craziness of rock 'n' roll.

My love for Charlane and the trees is as hard to express as my love for my family or for a good song. These things are so deep, I couldn't breathe if they weren't a part of my life.

Now, I know that not everyone has the temperament or the desire to be a tree farmer. But that doesn't mean that everyone, whether living in a city or in the suburbs, can't enjoy the benefits of trees and do their fair share to keep trees and forests alive and well.

WHAT CAN BE DONE?

There are so many things we all can do to help. We've discussed wood certification in earlier chapters. If that idea appeals to you, then by all means, when you go to the hardware or home building store make sure the wood you buy is certified. Just don't be fooled by the extremists who maintain that tree farming, or growing trees for commercial purposes, is a bad thing. In fact, it's a very good thing. We need those well managed forests for wood production.

Support companies and products that use recycled wood products. Today stationery, greeting cards, newspapers and other products are often made from recycled wood products, and that practice should be encouraged and supported not only with words but with our wallets. I've heard about other companies that take wood from houses and buildings that are being torn down and recycled into other uses. Right on!

Again, be a concerned, informed, and active consumer. Check out a company's environmental and recycling positions. Support companies that follow sound forest management practices, and that understand the big picture. It can be done and is being done.

I remember a quote from Sting, who is an involved advocate for the rain forests, to the effect that if he had no way to feed his family other than to cut down the trees in the rain forests, then he'd do it. He's right, but his point is that it doesn't have to come to that. Pay close attention to these issues, and make sure what you read about them is truthful. There are trouble spots in the world where our forests are concerned, and we need to know about those places and try to find intelligent, valid solutions to those problems. And where we can help, we need to do so.

A quick look on the Internet reveals various products being made from trees in rain forests, such as cosmetics and foods, in an environmentally friendly way. The Body Shop, an English-based cosmetics company, was perhaps the first to promote its practice of using extracts and products from the rain forests without destroying the trees. Ben & Jerry's Ice Cream also claims to use nuts from the rain forests, in part, to help save the trees. We've already talked about the medicinal value of these fabulous forests. We need to support these efforts. The more ways we can use the gifts of the forests without harming them, the better.

Be an informed voter. I know it can be time-consuming and often seems futile, but you can make a difference. Pay attention to forestry issues before you go into the voting booth, and consider the consequences of any changes in legislation. Make sure your vote lands on the right side of forestry debates. Consider our urban forests in land development plans, and beware of urban sprawl. Let's have *smart* growth, not just growth in and around our cites and urban areas.

Pick your battles. Every once in a while I'll read about a beautiful old tree being cut down to make way for a development, a road, or an easement. When these trees are threatened, sometimes a person who never thought about being a leader for a cause will step up and take a stand. And sometimes that's all it takes. Or a group of citizens might rally together, and simply by communicating with the developer, by suggesting a small alteration in his project design, a special tree can be saved. I think we can all admit that sometimes we do have to accept the removal of some trees for development purposes, but certainly there are the cases where some forethought and

creativity can save what might already be a beautiful landscape. Sometimes the battle to save a special tree is lost, but
even in these cases, the word gets out. It's worth the effort. We
need to learn to give consideration to the existing natural
landscape in our developments, whether residential, commercial, or otherwise.

There's also the issue of preserving land for future generations. Possible options include selling it to conservation
groups, or to the government as part of a public land expansion program. Or you might want to support laws that make
it easy for landowners to save their land from development but
reap the economic value from it. The Nature Conservancy, for
one, helps families find a way to donate land to a nonprofit or
governmental entity, yet still enjoy maximum income and
estate tax benefits.

Such options might appeal to those who own property they
no longer use or property that's highly appreciated, the sale of
which would result in a high capital gains tax burden; to families who have substantial real estate holdings and wish to
reduce their estate tax burden; to those who have heirs who
might not protect the land's conservation values; or those who
recognize that greater expertise is needed to protect and manage the land.

State and local governments often have land trust programs
available. It is not unusual for areas under strong development
to have local families band together to try to buy green space
and save it from development. In this day of urban sprawl, it's
heartwarming to know that people still value a place to sit and
relax under trees.

It's also important that our schools, churches and civic
groups play a role in the good stewardship of our American
forests. Schools can adopt a plot of land and make sure it is
well maintained. One school in Twiggs County, where I live,

created a nature trail on its grounds, and a vegetable and flower garden as well. Scout troops can plant trees and nurture them as a way of celebrating Arbor Day. Field trips to forests for plant identification, bird watching, and wildlife study are a wonderful idea. Youngsters can also go to see a well-managed tree farm, or a harvesting operation, or a saw or pulp mill to better understand forest use. This is especially important for those who live in metropolitan areas and may not have any concept of the stewardship of our natural resources. The Project Learning Tree (or PLT for short) program that exists throughout our country helps children to understand and think about outdoor issues. Many parents and educators are not even aware that this program exists, and it is one of the best ways of exposing our children to the world of nature. Other similar programs like Project WILD and Project WET are excellent as well. You can find out more about these programs by contacting them directly, and that information is in the references section of this book. The education of our children on the issues of sound forest use and conservation of all our natural resources is of paramount importance to America.

Of course, while you're at it, don't forget to plant trees on your own land, or in your own yard. They add so much beauty and will make a lasting difference, not to mention the monetary appreciation to your property.

Young people who have an interest in trees and the environment should be encouraged to consider forestry as a profession. There are many wonderful schools and universities, such as the Daniel B. Warnell School of Forest Resources at the University of Georgia, which offer excellent forestry instruction. Various career opportunities await those that graduate from these colleges and universities. Many farms and corporations employ consulting foresters. There are also careers in the Forest Service as well as positions in cities as towns for arborists and landscape architects. Educating others is yet another way of utilizing the knowledge gained from such institutions.

Research also plays a very important role in forestry. Through research we find ways to improve tree and forest health, increase the growth rates, and improve wildlife habitat.

Throughout this book, the message has been how important trees are to our way of life. Our forefathers used (and yes, sometimes abused) the trees and forests in order to build our great nation. We have a choice. We can successfully manage our prized trees and forests — or we can lose them. As we enter this new millennium with over six billion people on our planet, I think we are, on the whole, doing the right things. We must stay on this path.

All of us — forest products companies, consumers, manufacturers, farmers, environmentalists, naturalists, and users of recreational lands — must work together for the future of our forests.

When it comes to saving our forests, my old friends Keith and Mick may have put it best:

You can't always get what you want,
but if you try sometimes . . . you get what you need.

THE ART OF FORESTRY

One of my mother's favorite old sayings was, "There is an art to everything." It's so true. It doesn't matter if you are a mechanic, an athlete, a salesperson, a doctor, a clerk, a builder, an architect, a writer, or ever a rock 'n' roll piano player. Whatever you do, there is an art to it. There is certainly an art to forest and land management. And the thing that fascinates me – truly fascinates me – is that the canvas we use for the art of forestry is the landscape of our counties and rural areas, our cities, our states, our nation – indeed, the landscape of the world. So let's be careful of the brushstrokes we use on that canvas. Let's be careful of the colors we mix on our palette to use on that canvas. Because there is one thing for sure: the picture that we paint is something we will all be looking at for a long, long, time to come. And I know that all of us – you and I – want that picture to be nothing less than . . . a masterpiece.

APPENDIX

PERCs FOR THE FOREST

There is a wonderful organization based in Bozeman, Montana, called PERC. The letters stand for Political Economy Research Center. As the title indicates, it is first of all a research center. PERC is the nation's oldest and largest institute dedicated to original research that brings market principles to resolving environmental problems. This organization pioneered the approach known as free-market environmentalism. Their research is used by everyone from CNN to colleges and universities, and they also have a strong outreach through conferences, books and environmental education. They advocate that private ownership coupled with entrepreneural sprit equals a winning combination for the environment. The publications they produce cover a wide range of environmental concerns, from forestry to fisheries to grassland leases and more, and cover issues from environmental economics to private property rights. Their approach to stewardship of our natural resources has resulted in many interesting and creative ideas and concepts. I would recommend that anyone interested should contact them and investigate their offerings. They can be reached at:

PERC
502 SOUTH 19th AVE.
BOSEMAN, MT 59718
(406) 5879591
Website: www.perc.org

SUGGESTED WEBSITES

American Forest Foundation – www.forestfoundation.org

American Forest & Paper Association – www.afandpa.org

American Forests – www.americanforests.org

American Tree Farm System – www.treefarmsystem.org

Association of Consulting Foresters of America – www.acf-foresters.com

Cradle of Forestry in America Interpretive Assn. – www.cradleofforestry.com

EcoForestry Institute – www.geocities.com/geoforests

Forest History Society – www.lib.duke.edu/forest

Forest Landowners Association – www.ag.auburn.edu/grassroots/flai

Forest Landowners Tax Council – www.forestlandowners.com/taxcouncil.html

Forest Resources Association Inc. – www.apulpa.org

Global Association of Online Foresters – www.foresters.org

International Society of Arborculture – www.isa-arbor.com

National Association of State Foresters – www.stateforesters.org

National Council of Private Forests – www.pinchot.org/pic/farmbill/ncpf.pdg

National Woodland Owners Association – www.woodlandowners.org

Pinchot Institute for Conservation – www.pinchot.org

Project Learning Tree – www.plt.org

Society of American Foresters – www.safnet.org

The Forestry Site – www.forestry.com

Trees for Tomorrow – www.treesfortomorrow.com

USDA/Cooperative State Research, Education & Ext. Service – www.reeusda.gov

SUGGESTED READING

American Forests, by Douglas W. MacCleery. USDA Forest Service: Washington D.C., 1992.

America's Ancient Forests: From the Ice Age to the Age of Discovery, by Thomas M. Bonnicksen. John Wiley and Sons, 1999.

America's Wild Woodlands, by the National Geographic Society. Washington, D.C., 1985.

Americans and Their Forests: A Historical Geography, by Michael Williams. Cambridge University Press, 1989.

The Biography of a Tree, by James P. Jackson. Jonathan David: Middle Village, N.Y., 1979.

Breaking New Ground, by Gifford Pinchot. Island Press: Washington D.C.,1947.

Enchanted Canopy, by Andrew W. Mitchell. Macmillan: New York, 1986.

Facts, Not Fear: Teaching Children about the Environment, by Michael Sanera and Jane S. Shaw. Regnery Publishing: Washington D.C. 1999.

Forest Resource Economics and Finance, by W. David Klemperer. McGraw-Hill: New York, 1996.

Forest Resources Policy, by Paul V. Ellefson. McGraw-Hill: New York, 1992.

The Green America Book, by the American Forest Institute. Washington, D.C., 1980.

Green Spirit: Trees Are the Answer, by Patrick Moore. Greenspirit Enterprises: Vancouver, B.C., Canada.

A Guide to Smart Growth: Shattering Myths, Providing Solutions, by Jane S. Shaw and Ronald D. Utt, eds. Heritage Foundation: Washington, D.C.

Ortho's All About Trees, by Jan Johnsen, et al. Ortho Books: San Ramon, Calif., 1982.

Simon and Schuster's Guide to Trees, by Paola Lanzara and Mariella Pizzetti. Simon and Schuster: New York, 1977.

Southern National Forests, by Sharyn Kane and Richard Keeton. Falcon Press: Helena, Mont. 1993.

Sustainability of Temperate Forests, by Roger A. Sedjo, Alberto Goetzl and Steverson O. Moffat. Resources for the Future: Washington D.C.,1965.

This Is a Tree, by Ross E. Hutchins. Dodd, Mead: New York, 1964.

Trees, by the Chicago Botanic Garden and the Holden Arboretum. Pantheon Books: New York, 1996.

Tropical Forest, by Mary Bratten. Thomas Y. Crowell: New York, 1973.

Tropical Rainforests, by James D. Nations. Franklin Watts: New York, 1998.

A Walk in the Forest, by Albert List Jr. and Ilka List. Thomas Y. Crowell: New York, 1977.

Wild Lands for Wildlife, by Noel Grove. National Geographic Society: Washington D.C., 1984.